THE FRONTIERS
OF SCIENCE AND MEDICINE

THE
FRONTIERS
OF SCIENCE
AND MEDICINE

edited by
Rick J. Carlson

Henry Regnery Company·Chicago

Contents

Preface

A new medicine is needed: the limits of today's medicine have been reached, even surpassed.

Over the last few years, perhaps more so in the United States where medicine has fashioned a technological palace, attitudes towards medicine have changed. A few years ago the suggestion that the limits of medicine had been reached would have met disbelief, even derision. Today it is a matter of degree. Today, also, the need for a more holistic medicine is rapidly being recognized. But conceptualizing the limits of modern medicine is several steps short of creating a new medicine. The task is enormous and is complicated by the lack of clear ideas. But there are some signs. The raw materials appear, often spontaneously, but the job remains one of paradigm-building. New approaches to health – a new paradigm – must be carefully fashioned.

In May 1974 a conference and lecture programme, 'The May Lectures , was held in London. The explicit purpose of the programme was to begin to build a new medicine – one more closely calibrated with human needs. This was done by linking together a series of presentations and lectures which represented potential elements of a new science and, in turn, a new medicine. The brush stroke was very broad – in part because little is known, but also because today's medicine is too narrow and exclusive. Tomorrow's medicine will undoubtedly be broader and more inclusive.

The May Lectures programme was only a beginning. Much more needs to be done. A 'sequel' to the May Lectures programme has just been held in the United States. To facilitate even more activity, these proceedings have been prepared.

This book is more than a series of essays loosely strung together. First, a lengthy essay introduces the subject and weaves together the themes treated in the essays that follow. And at the end of the book, an analytic summary of the lectures by a journalist who covered the programme for *BRES,* a journal published in the Netherlands, provides some fascinating insights. In addition, 'cement' has been placed between each essay to create a larger conceptual framework, and to provide reasonably coherent transitions. Finally, each essay has been edited to omit extraneous material. The flavour of the individual presentations has been retained wherever possible, although in some cases just excerpts are included. Nevertheless, the narrative is not from one hand. There are leaps and bounds, unevenness and even roughness. But the whole is more than the sum of the parts.

CHAPTER I

The End of Medicine and the Beginning of Health

We have reached, perhaps surpassed, the limits of modern medicine to produce health. Medicine can and does cure; but if it is health that we care about, then a new approach to health – together with a new medicine – will have to be fashioned. Modern medicine must be largely abandoned (some of it to be resurrected) because it enslaves the resources needed to produce health.

The Beginning of the End

In tests at the Menninger Clinic in Kansas, Chief Rolling Thunder, a Shoshone medicine man, was asked to 'cure' a contusion on a subject's leg. The Chief employed one of his favourite methods. He placed his mouth over and around the bruise, sucked vigorously, and then dashed to the other side of the room and vomited. The bruise disappeared at roughly the same time that the 'scientists' in the room rushed to retrieve the vomit. This is a perceptual problem. To the scientists, the 'cure' could only have been effected if the damaged tissue in the bruised leg had somehow been physically extracted. Of course, it was not 'removed' in the sense in which the scientists could understand it. But the bruise disappeared. And the 'explanation' probably lies in perception. To the subject and the Chief, the sucking and the vomiting were elements of drama underpinning a 'belief' system – a belief that a 'cure' could be achieved. The Chief simply perceived the episode differently, and the explanation for the cure may lie in this perceptual difference.

Perceptual differences lie at the heart of the problem. The public simply believes that medicine produces health. As a result, nearly all our resources and energy are expended in providing medical care. And the price is high – so the costs have been shifted to governments.

Within this decade a national health insurance plan will be adopted in the United States. A national health service has existed in Great Britain since 1946. The approaches are different. A health insurance plan underwrites the costs of care provided by physicians and hospitals; a health service 'nationalizes' the physicians by employing them and the hospitals by absorbing them. But, while different, the consequences of both 'plans' are the same. First, care – a specified set of medical benefits – is ensured for all, or at least most, citizens. Second, existing approaches to health are stabilized, even entrenched. This is retrograde. There is sound theory and accumulating evidence that medical care – of the type that the National Health Service and national health insurance programme pay for – has relatively little impact on health and, as time passes, is likely to have even less.

The Effectiveness of Medicine

There is not much – either effectiveness or evidence. There has, however, been some work on the 'quality' of care. The studies that have been done show that medical care is very uneven and, in some cases, poor.[1] For example, the rates for the performance of many procedures vary wildly from one area to another – hysterectomy success rates vary as much as ten to one from one region in the United States to another. This is not surprising: medicine is a human undertaking, and human error naturally occurs. But the way medicine is practised creates conditions in which error thrives: the pace is frantic and powerful drugs and tools are brandished. The patient, then, is surrounded by machines with rough edges and healers with little time.

If there is not much research on quality, there is even less squarely focused on 'effectiveness' – what does medicine *do* for patients? In the United States, Robert Brook has launched some of the most stinging salvos,[2] and in Great Britain A. L. Cochrane's book *Effectiveness and Efficiency*[3] is perhaps the most trenchant examination of the question.

Both Brook and Cochrane find that much of medicine, if measured in terms of clinical effectiveness – the 'outcome' to the patient – is not related to what happens to the patient. To put it simply, much of what is done by doctors and hospitals cannot be shown to contribute to the outcome of care to the patient.

Take one of Brook's studies as an example. The 'outcomes' of 141 emergency room patients were examined. Initially, only 94 out of the 141 patients completed the battery of studies based on diagnostic X-rays; 77 (or 55 per cent) received an adequate workup based on the intern's diagnostic impression; but only 37 out of 98 patients, having received diagnostic X-ray examinations, were informed whether the result was normal or abnormal; and only 14 out of the 38 patients with abnormal X-ray results (or 37 per cent) appear to have received adequate therapy for the condition indicated. Thus, the study resulted in effective medical care for only 38 patients (or 27 per cent) and ineffective care for 84 patients (or 60 per cent); and there was neither effective nor ineffective care for 19 patients (or the remaining 13 per cent).

The study was not conducted in a small rural hospital, nor in the often inadequate and shabby facilities of many major public hospitals. Rather, the study took place in the Baltimore City Hospital emergency room, where it was assumed that the competence and efficiency of the house staff would be high. Over ninety per cent of the medical resident staff at the time were affiliated with the highly regarded Johns Hopkins University School of Medicine, and were graduates of American medical schools.

It is one thing to look at what medicine can do for the patient. But another, perhaps more important, question is what is the 'relative' impact of medicine compared to other factors. Unfortunately, there have been just a handful of studies comparing medicine with the other factors such as air quality, nutrition, education, etc.[6] However, the studies uniformly demonstrate that improvements in health can be more readily achieved if resources are diverted from medical care into other programmes.

Medical care is limited – it 'produces' less health than is generally understood. But it can also damage. For instance,

one in every eighteen patients admitted to hospital con-
tracts an infection while hospitalized.[5] Other studies suggest
that roughly twenty-five per cent of all hospital admissions
are due to injuries incurred by patients while receiving care.
And finally, in a major study of medical malpractice, a
commission of the United States government concluded that
at least seven per cent of the contacts patients have with
medical care result in injuries that are serious enough to
justify a law suit[6].

Ivan Illich, in a recently published book entitled *Medical
Nemesis*,[7] takes the argument a few steps further. To Illich the
problem is not just negligence – or even the unintended
effects of prudently provided care. The 'fault', instead, is
inherent in medicine. Medical care to Illich has become too
complicated, too large and too mechanistic – its very
ponderousness strips it of the capacity to heal. There are too
many rough and clumsy edges to wound the patients caught
up in it. Beyond this, monopoly power strips the patients of
both the tools and the responsibility to care for themselves.
Illich's remedy is to set limits to institutional size and
rapacity.[8] And he argues that in medicine those limits have
long since been reached.

The Public Response

In Great Britain, the National Health Service threatens to
bankrupt the social services budget. The National Health
Service was created in order to improve the health of the
population sufficiently so as to lessen demand, and hence to
reduce the costs of care. But the opposite has occurred. And
the reasons are simple: medical care does not reduce
demand; it creates it by fostering dependency. And it fails to
improve the health of the population because medical care
only episodically and rarely influences health. The factors
which do influence health are generally not considered to be
within the jurisdiction of medicine. In short, the wrong
programmes are financed if it is health that is sought.

In the United States medicine, because it is private, faces
fewer budget restrictions. And it is more sophisticated.
Hence, it is pushed to greater extremes. But the United
States is none the less about to ringingly endorse modern

medicine, despite mounting evidence of its ineffectiveness, by the passage of a national health insurance programme.

The populations of both the United Kingdom and the United States are no longer getting healthier. Morbidity and mortality scales show that improvements in health have reached a plateau. In fact, white male longevity is decreasing in the United States. The powerful impact on health of social and environmental factors – such as the quality of air and water, the level of stress and noise, and so on – is largely ignored. The air we breathe undeniably induces disease and disability. Stress ravages many whose work, and even recreation, compel them to endure it. And many of the foods and beverages we consume are contaminated. But medicine does not deal with any of these factors. Medicine continues to focus on the cure of the human animal whose environment is destroying him. Yet the United States pays an enormous price for medical care – over $100,000,000,000 – despite the fact that those resources might be allocated to secure more health and fewer 'cures'.

The 'Relativity' of Medicine

The medicine of Great Britain and the United States is very new. Hospitals, in the sense in which we now use the word, were virtually unknown until the late nineteenth century. And the scientific foundations of medicine were only put into place in the first two decades of this century. Sepsis and medicinals are contemporary tools. The medicine we have is 'modern' despite the fact that some of its roots lie in the past.

Our approach to health is premised upon a set of medical theories which differ from those in other parts of the world. In the West, medical care is oriented towards 'curing' rather than either prevention of disease or its melioration through interventions in the social and environmental orders to deter or delay its onset. Medical care in the United States is probably the most elaborate form of allopathic medicine, with that in Great Britain close behind. But allopathy is only one theory, or set of theories, upon which medicine can be based. To oversimplify, allopathy operates on the assumption that the treatment of disease is dependent upon the elimination of its symptoms. Thus modern medicine uses techniques such as surgery and chemotherapy which extirpate symptoms but which do not deal with the basic and underlying causes of disease and ill-health. A patient's stomach ulcers might be surgically removed but, upon discharge from the hospital, the patient resumes the lifestyle that produced the ulcers – the patient is discharged, the diseased organ goes to the pathologist, the doctor goes to the bank, and the patient goes to the pub.

Allopathy can be contrasted with at least two other approaches to illustrate the relativity of medical practice. One approach, found at the margins of medical care in almost all places in the world, is homoeopathy. The goal of homoeopathy is to restore health, principally through the use of chemical agents in the treatment drawn from the same agents which induced the disease in the first place. A second example is psychic healing or the laying on of hands. While often classified (and denigrated as well) as 'faith healing', recent research by Dr Bernard Grad at Montreal, Sister Justa Smith,[9] and others, as well as changes recorded in both healers' and patients' coronas by Kirlian photography,[10] indicate that an as yet undefinable form of 'energy' appears to pass from healer to patient, which in some cases restores physiology and function. This does not mean that a positive attitude by the patient does not help regardless of the system of medicine used. The work of Jerome Frank, among others, demonstrates that positive attitudes by patients enhance healing.[11]

There is one further example which illustrates the difference in medical theories in a more concrete way. The demonstrable success of acupuncture as an analgesic agent undercuts the allopathic pain theory – that is, that pain is specific to the area of the body which is supposedly its source; that pain in the shoulder, for example, reflects the presence of pathology in that area. In acupuncture practice, pain is a function of imbalances in the body's energy system. Acupuncture seems to work through a form of 'bioenergy' much in the same way as psychic healing; an energy which is said by the Chinese to flow through twelve meridians in the body. Since these meridians have not been fully described, it is assumed that they do not exist and that the

Chinese do not understand how acupuncture works. There are theories and explanations but, because they do not 'fit' prevailing Western theories, they have been poorly understood and too quickly rejected. This is just plain chauvinism and bias. There is no universally accepted theory of anaesthesia in allopathic practice. To quote Andrew Weil, author of *The Natural Mind*:

> ... Although anesthesia has been around for over a hundred years and although millions of persons have been put into the state under close observation, no satisfactory theory of general anesthesia exists; doctors have no idea what these drugs do to the brain that accounts for the state.[12]

Our medicine then is relative, not absolute. Nevertheless, we do not question whether there are other ways, other means, to provide medical care. Even more fundamentally, we rarely examine the relationship or correspondences between the care that is delivered and the health of the population. The reasons for this are many and complex, but among them is a simple one: we have equated medicine with health. And the price we pay is clear: failing health and exorbitant costs.

The Technological Fix

There are many ways to achieve health. And historically there have been many varieties of medicine. Each has had varying success in the generation and maintenance of health. Today, in most Western nations, we have one kind of medicine – allopathy. This species of medicine has three fundamental premises: first, that disease is not complex and (its symptoms) can be extirpated by specific probes into the body; second, that the body is a machine and, since all machines are essentially alike, patients with like symptoms can be treated alike; and third, that health is the product of medical care services, specific to a given disease.

The result is the engineering of health – the assumption that health is the result of the well-oiled functioning of the body's parts. This requires the identification and classification of malfunctions in bodily machinery. This has, in turn, two consequences. The first is industrialization. Medicine classifies diseases to match the 'needs' of its consumers; creates specific products to meet those needs, including drugs, surgery and prosthesis; creates a delivery system to transfer those products to the patients, featuring the hospital as the major outlet; and obtains its promotion, market analyses and financing from the private insurance sector and increasingly the Federal Government. If together they are willing to spend $100,000,000,000 on medical care, then the dependent consumer is easily convinced that the route to health is paved with doctors.

The second consequence is medicine's fascination with disease. The most incisive example is the hospital. The purpose of the hospital is to classify, confine and immobilize. Admission is contingent on appropriate classification of a disease condition. The patient is then confined in quarters that are virtually the same everywhere. This is because to the physician the human being is simply a machine with interchangeable parts. A given disease can be treated identically in Wales or Washington – it is the 'disease' that is being treated, not the person. This also accounts for the 'immobilization' of the patient. Apart from its convenience to the harried doctor, immobilization is the same as turning off the engine of a car and leaving it in a garage: the car and the human are both machines in need of repair.

But there is more to it than this. While we do not know enough about what produces health, we do know some things – commonsense things. For example, we know that a nutritious diet, recreation, fresh air and sunlight are related to health. But because the hospital is a factory for the repair of disease, none of these things are readily available. Hospital food is not only tasteless, it is distinctly unnutritious – nothing fresh, everything frozen, white bread, butter, and so on. There·is no opportunity for recreation and exercise in a hospital – there could be gyms and exercise rooms – and someone doing yoga or any other bodily exercise faces derision, even prohibition. And there is little opportunity to be outdoors; hospitals are hermetically sealed chambers – the only way a patient can get outdoors (if there is any 'outdoors') is to grope to the front door and then face the possibility of alarm from the nurses at the admission desk. The modern hospital is one of the unhealthiest places around.

Today's medicine is a technological fix – it has driven itself into a cul-de-sac. It can produce cures for some individuals, although an increasing proportion of those who seek services are worse off for their trouble. But it is no longer producing health for a population beset by post-industrial traumas. Modern medicine is not modern – it is suited to industrial populations; populations for which sanitary services have raised the threshold of health and drugs have removed the ravages of infection. But in today's post-industrial culture patients are not decimated by germs; they are ravaged by stress and anxiety, contaminated by processed foods, surrounded by gadgetry that takes the meaning out of work and play, and physically atrophied by spectatorism and desk jobs. A new medicine must confront these problems. Bones will still break and need to be set, but the new medicine must rediscover the routes to health.

CHAPTER II

A New Paradigm?

The doctor said: this-and-that indicates that this-and-that is wrong with you, but if an analysis of this-and-that does not confirm our diagnosis, we must suspect you of having this-and-that. If we assume that you have this-and-that, then . . . and so on. There was only one question Ivan Illyich wanted answered: was his condition dangerous or not? But the doctor ignored that question as irrelevant. From the doctor's point of view, such a question was unworthy of consideration. One had only to weigh possibilities: floating kidneys, chronic catarrh, or an ailment of the caecum. There was no question of the life of Ivan Illyich – nothing but a contest between floating kidneys and the caecum. In the presence of Ivan Illyich the doctor gave a brilliant solution of the problem in favour of the caecum, with the reservation that the analysis of his water might supply new information necessitating a reconsideration of the case.[1]

We only know a few things about health. We know that modern medicine is intrinsically flawed. And many of us sense that a new medicine is emerging, as we perceive a new culture emerging. But we are at a threshold – we can see behind us very clearly, but looking towards the future is more difficult.

Medicine and Science

Phenomena which do not fit prevailing moulds are often rejected as 'unscientific'. This is also true in medicine – in part because medicine is considered to be part of science. But this is not strictly accurate. There are elements of modern medicine, particularly biomedical research, which adhere to principles of scientific inquiry. But fundamentally, the practice of medicine is an alloy of art, hunch, science and a lot of slavish adherence to dogma. Nevertheless, unconventional healing techniques and bioenergetics are debunked because they are not sufficiently 'scientific'. Lawrence LeShan, a psychologist, in his new book *The Medium, the Mystic and the Physicist*, borrowing from Carington, offers two reasons why this is the case:

> Carington . . . felt that there were 2 main reasons for the rejection by scientists: 1) that its introduction is perceived as weakening the status of causality and law in science; 2) that "the way will be opened for the introduction in thin disguise of all the magic and superstition which they have fought against so hard and long."[2]

But science is bluffing; there is no body of inviolate knowledge; reality is relative. Only a few centuries ago, the king of France entrusted his military might to a sixteen-year-old girl who heard voices from God.

Arthur Koestler, in his recent work *The Roots of Coincidence*, like LeShan traces the convergence of physics and mysticism. Physics long ago abandoned mechanistic conceptions of reality and has since plunged into what must be called a kind of mysticism. How else can you describe a 'neutrino' or a 'quark'? He quotes Henry Marganau, Professor of Physics at Yale:

> Towards the end of the last century the view arose that all interactions involved material objects. This is no longer held to be true. We now know that there are fields which are wholly non-material. The quantum mechanical interactions of physical psi fields – interestingly and perhaps amusingly the physicist's psi has a certain abstractness and vagueness of interpretation in common with the parapsychologist's psi – these interactions are wholly non-material, yet they are described by the most important and the most basic equations of present-day quantum mechanics. These equations say nothing about masses moving; they regulate the behavior of very abstract fields often as tenuous as the square root of a probability.[3]

Indifferent to change around it, medicine tenaciously clings to the mechanistic model. But as science continues to evolve, medicine may have to loosen its grip. What are some of the elements of a 'new science' – which in turn may infuse the medicine of the future?

The Center for the Study of Social Policy at Stanford Research Institute recently completed an examination of 'changing images of man'. Their report offers six axioms to characterize the classical view of science:[4]

Reason is the supreme tool of man.

Knowledge, acquired through the use of reason, will free mankind from ignorance and will lead to a better future.

The universe is inherently orderly and physical.

This order can be discovered by science and objectively expressed.

Only science deals in empirically verifiable truth.

Observation and experimentation are the only valid means of discovering scientific truth, which is always independent of the observer.[5]

The ground under these axioms is shaking – each is under challenge. One of the essays in this volume – Lyall Watson's discussion of psychic surgery – articulates a general critique. But there are arguments against each.

Axioms One and Two

To some the flaw is inherent in the use of 'reason' for problem-solving. To quote Barry Commoner:

There is, indeed, a specific fault in our system of science, and in the resultant understanding of the natural world which, I believe, helps to explain the ecological failure of technology. This fault is reductionism, the view that effective understanding of a complex system can be achieved by investigating the properties of its isolated parts. The reductionist methodology, which is so characteristic of much of modern research, is not an effective means of analyzing the vast natural systems that are threatened by degradation.[6]

Reason has steadily ascended since the Greeks. In its mildest applications it is a useful tool for conventional problem-solving, even though its use often precludes consideration of factors which inevitably influence the result. The increasing awareness of scientists that their own attitudes and motivations can influence the results of their experimental work is an example.[7] But at its worst it is transformed into dogma which leads to inflexibility and slavishness. Is it 'reasonable' to expect that schools, freely available to all, will necessarily teach us to be wise? And is it necessarily 'reasonable' for us to assume that honourable men and women assembling together to debate and discuss issues of policy will always reach sound and equitable conclusions? Reason can be a useful tool, but it is foolish to assume that human minds, through the use of reason alone, can be wholly responsible for the evolution of the species. Jonas Salk examines this question in his book *The Survival of the Wisest,* and concludes that the species is doomed if we stay on the rationalistic trajectory we are on. Consequently he argues for the further 'evolution' of human consciousness – a consciousness which transcends human reason:

> ... [A] new body of conscious individuals exists expressing its desire for a better life for Man as a species and as individuals, eager to devote themselves to this end. Such groups, when they are able to coalesce through an understanding of their relatedness to one another and to the natural processes involved in 'Nature's game' of survival and evolution, will find strength and courage in sensing themselves as a part of the Cosmos and as being involved in a game that is in accord with Nature and not anti-natural. These groups will initiate movements, which in turn will be manifest in their effect not only upon the species and the planet but upon individual lives. Their benefit is likely to be expressed in a greater satisfaction and fulfilment in life.[8]

Axiom Three

Today's physics is inconsistent with this proposition. Sir

James Jeans ties it up in one frequently repeated quotation:

> Today there is a wide measure of agreement, which on
> the physical side of science approaches almost to
> unanimity, that the stream of knowledge is heading
> towards a non-mechanical reality; the universe begins
> to look more like a great thought than like a great
> machine.[9]

Axioms Four and Five

Slowly we are recognizing that our reality is only a 'consensus reality'. Werner Erhard devotes much of his essay to this subject. And Carlos Castaneda makes the point in a dialogue on reality between don Juan and himself in his new book, *Tales of Power:*

> "You like the humbleness of a beggar," he said softly.
> "You bow your head to reason."
> "I always think that I'm being tricked," I said. "That's
> the crux of my problem."
> "You're right. You are being tricked," he retorted with
> a disarming smile. "That cannot be your problem. The
> real crux of the matter is that you feel that I am
> deliberately lying to you, am I correct?"
> "Yes. There is something in myself that doesn't let me
> believe that what's taking place is real."
> "You're right again. Nothing of what is taking place is
> real."
> "What do you mean by that, don Juan?"
> "Things are real only after one has learned to agree on
> their realness. What took place this evening, for
> instance, cannot possibly be real to you, because no one
> could agree with you about it."
> "Do you mean that you didn't see what happened?"
> "Of course I did. But I don't count. I am the one who's
> lying to you, remember?"
> ". . . Think for a moment. Can you deviate from the
> path that they've lined up for you? No. Your thoughts
> are fixed forever in their terms. That is slavery. I, on the
> other hand, brought you freedom. Freedom is expen-

sive, but the price is not impossible. So, fear your
captors, your masters. Don't waste your time and your
power fearing me."
I knew that he was right, and yet in spite of my genuine
agreement with him I also knew that my life-long habits
would make me stick to my old path. I did indeed feel
like a slave.[10]

Despite the power of this passage, our accepted notions of
'reality' are hard to shake. Altered states of consciousness,
whether drug-induced or not, reveal to the subject that
reality has many dimensions – and that consensus reality is
only that dimension of which we are most frequently conscious. This is not to say that one dimension of reality is
necessarily more valid, but only that reality is relative, not
absolute.

Axiom Six

There are two emerging concepts which undermine this
point. First, since the postulation of the uncertainty principle
by Heisenberg, it has become clear that there is no such
thing as an 'independent observer'. The investigator is always
a part of the experiment. Second, the axiom leaves out the
role of 'experience'. Knowledge is arid without experience: a
man cannot know the pains and pleasures of childbirth; a
person who has not climbed a mountain cannot 'know' what
it is to do so. There is a kind of knowledge engendered out
of experience; it is the kind of knowledge that Roszak
characterizes as 'that [which] must come through the body
and be accepted on the body's own terms as a lesson not to
be learned elsewhere or otherwise: an organic message,
organically integrated.'[11]

In the future our science will have to assimilate new information, as rigorously as it now resists it. We are at 'boundary
conditions' in science today. To some, an age of mysticism is
upon us; to others, science is simply slowly shifting its base
– towards the integration of new information. This, after all,
is what science is all about – adaptation under the impress
of new ideas, new evidence and new thinking. Whatever the

means, a paradigm shift in scientific inquiry will necessarily influence medicine.

A New Paradigm for Medicine

We are at the point of a paradigm shift in medicine. Our perceptions of health and the systems we construct out of those perceptions are calibrated with our larger perceptions of the world around us. If this is so, a reconstruction of where we have been and where we are should aid us in speculating about the future – a new paradigm and a new medicine.

In a very rough sense, medicine has passed through six eras to the present. Each of these eras can be examined in three steps: first by characterizing the dominant world-view relating to health; second by identifying the most utilized medical technologies; and finally by adducing the prevailing health paradigm, which can be seen as an amalgam of the world-view and the technology. An analysis of these eras will generate some of the elements of a new paradigm for health in the future.

The Greeks and the Romans

To the Greeks, and to a lesser extent the Romans, the world presented endless opportunities. Progress was to be made by accumulating knowledge. The world could be mastered through rationality – the application of reason to problem-solving. Excellence was the goal, at least for the citizens of Athens.[12] Health was a goal too; but it was also seen, more importantly, as a process – a way of living. Health was almost synonymous with excellence – both the body and the mind could be trained to achieve excellence. Training was an individual matter, so health was a matter of individual responsibility. The human was not a victim of capricious powers as the 'barbarians' surrounding the empire believed. Health then was not a function of luck and superstition; it could be rationally pursued. Each individual could tune his body to perfection, could eat well, but moderately, and could balance this by shaping his mind. Moderation was pivotal. The Greeks believed that life should be enjoyed, but in moderation.

Greek medicine flowed naturally from these views of the

world. An integral feature of Greek medicine was careful observation. This was coupled with what we would characterize today as humanistic medical practice – love and caring for the patient. One of the maxims of the Hippocratic School was 'where there is love of man, there is also love for the art.' This approach to health compelled rejection of past practices: 'All the unnatural phenomena of mysticism, magic, and astrology were put on one side as impediments to rational, scientific thinking about the problem of illness'.[13]

The Greeks also created a rudimentary public health practice. The links between exercise, diet, water quality and so on were comprehended. But here, as well as in the practices of the Hippocratic School, the technology was crude in contemporary terms. The Greeks were unaware of the workings of the body, although they took advantage of the carcasses and body parts sundered in combat to try to learn. But though crude, their technology was rational and subtle. They had a firm understanding of the self-limiting nature of disease. Medical practice, therefore, centred on the creation of a healing environment, the prescription of nourishment and exercise, and the influence of family, friends and lovers.

Both diagnosis and prognosis, because of the emphasis on close observation, were highly developed. Many descriptions and classifications of disease found in the Greek lexicons match those of today. Yet, at the theoretical level, Greek medicine was hollow – it had no sense of biodynamics, the infectious disease process, sepsis, surgery or chemotherapy. Its strength lay in its sound praxis – observation and assistance in recuperation. But its very strength contained the seeds of a subsequent perversion.

If moderation was the key to health for the Greeks, excess was the response by the Romans. Medical practice in the Roman Empire incorporated the principles of Greek medicine, and some of its schools of healing – particularly that of Galen – built upon the Greek example. The Romans advanced the anatomical arts by their greater curiosity in the limbs and organs jettisoned in combat; but they disdained the healing arts. In the highly stratified Roman society, healers, often of foreign extraction, were distrusted. A few physicians, occupying acceptable social strata, practised their trade, but to the Roman citizen illness was often preferable to the services of the lesser-born. To the Roman, then, medicine was a profoundly theoretical undertaking. What was observation of patients for the purpose of prognosis and healing to the Greeks became classification of diseases to add to the fund of human knowledge to the Romans. The roots of the medicine of the Middle Ages had been planted.

During the great empires of the Greek and Roman cultures, medicine moved out of mysticism into a consensus reality called rational. The paradigm of its medicine was squarely based on observing the patient, describing symptoms and behaviour, and (at least among the Greeks) aiding the patient to aid himself. Health then was a marriage of natural wisdom with rational wisdom – the rationality of medicine for the Greeks grew organically out of an understanding of the 'connections' between the species and Nature, even if its theoretical base was faulty. To the Romans, however, rationality started to emerge as a singular goal uncoupled from practice. In the centuries that followed, rationality became an end in itself.

The Ages of Magic

The medicine of the Greeks, and to some extent the Romans, was a lucid interval in the history of medical care. Medicine before the Greeks and the medicine that emerged after the fall of the Roman Empire shared some common conceptual ground – a trust in magic – although there were differences. The ages of magic that preceded the Greek and Roman empires, and those that immediately followed them, were conceptually consistent but yet different from the Middle Ages.

There are two kinds of magic. The first, unadulterated by 'reason', exists in a pure state. In this form it is a vision of reality without observation. The subject and the object are less clearly separated – in the sense in which reality is generally perceived today in the West. The other kind of magic grows paradoxically out of reason – when reason is stretched into a thinner and thinner substance. Thus, prior to the Greeks, the number of teeth in a horse's mouth may not have been known because to some cultures the horse was a sacred animal, not to be tampered with. This is a pure form of magic. But in the Middle Ages, when the horse was not considered sacred, the number of teeth in a horse's mouth could not be known with certainty because to look was absurd: formulations based on identification and classification of species 'equestrian' were available in texts – empirical verification was unnecessary. This is reason 'stretched' into magic. Both views are magical in the sense that direct 'observation' is not needed, because it is either sacrilegious or unnecessary.

The magic which characterized the Middle Ages, then, was a function of the religious mysticism of the times. Its medicine was similarly steeped in the same kind of mysticism. Direct observation and even empirically based healing was out-of-bounds. To the Christian, sickness and ill-health were the natural consequents of sin – efficacious cures grounded in pagan beliefs were affronts to the faith. But despite this zeal and this unique conception of magic, the medicine of this age was consistent with earlier ages. Each was dependent on the human's relationship with the gods.

The medicine which preceded the Greeks and Romans and that which prevailed thereafter until the eighteenth century, despite differences in prevailing views of reality, reflected the vicissitudes of man's relationships to the gods and to Nature. Sickness and disease resulted from disharmonies in these relationships. These disharmonies arose from many causes, but chief among them was behaviour which was offensive to the gods. To the pagan this was due to disharmony with his peculiar gods, however reified. To the Christian as well, disharmony, thought of as sin, lay at the root of the problem. These ideas appear to be simple. To some extent they are, but they were integral to the view of reality that prevailed. The world was a combat zone for the forces of good and evil. It was the species' task, unarmed with modern technology, to survive by alignment with benign forces and avoidance of the malignant. This required, among other things, attention to natural rhythms and harmonies. Hence, planting and reaping, birth and death, ritual and ceremony had all to 'fit' into natural patterns which, by their very nature, could not be altered. Health was seen to be the product of the best 'fit' and illness resulted when the individual or the society was 'out-of-phase', or in disharmony with the forces and rhythms of life.

The technology matched the ideas. There were three central elements. The first was the oral record. This ostensibly mythical body of tradition contained 'lessons' about the healthy life, frequently larded with references to the means and methods by which harmony, and in turn health, was to be maintained. The second – rituals – sprang from the first, although frequently 'repugnant' curative practices were incorporated. The rituals were not always arbitrary; most of them were based upon empirical observations of the surrounding world.

Sacrifice was the third element. This occasionally entailed human or animal sacrifice as a means of propitiating the gods – as, for example, in the tradition of some Central American cultures. Propitiation was a means of re-establishing a balance or harmony which, in the view of the society, had been upset. If the sacrifice was successful, presumably health would be the result – not just for an individual but for the society as well.

Self-sacrifice was also important. Individuals or groups, presumably responsible for the affliction, subjected themselves to regimens designed to please or pacify the 'management'.

The composer, arranger and conductor of these practices was the shaman. The shaman is a generic historical figure in most pre-modern cultures. Most shamans played three major roles. The first was to 'interpret' the significance of environmental perturbations, the second was to heal the patient and the third was to 'heal' the community.

The environment impinged brutally and directly upon pre-industrial cultures. The plastic and mortar which encase us now were not available then for protection. Moreover, there were no known techniques for taming Nature, which we assume we can do today. But since harmony with the environment was crucial to the health of both the individual and the culture, the 'messages' of the environment – the sun, the clouds, the storms and the seasons – were interpreted by the shaman for the larger community. The 'codes' that developed were invaluable parts of the technology the shaman brought to his work.

In his healing role with patients, the shaman emphasized the symbolic aspects of healing – including the use of colourful regalia, sacrifices, spitting of blood, the use of fire, and so on. In this aspect of his practice, the shaman was a colourful predecessor of the physician of today. But 'sickness' was also an event which could be used to instruct the larger community. Hence, the shaman also organized cultural experiences for the community, often around the sickness of a member. These 'group healing ceremonies', as Jerome Frank calls them, mixed curative acts – such as pulse readings – with culturally significant rituals.[14] The effect, if the shaman was skilful and perhaps lucky, was double – the patient was cured and the community was welded more tightly together and to the shaman.

Shamanism is an historical tradition, not a phenomenon peculiar to a given era. The term 'shaman' was not always used, but most historical periods possessed shaman-like traditions. In the Middle Ages – one of the ages of magic – the closest approximation was the healing monk. The monk, like the shaman centuries earlier, simply lacked the tools of healing that characterize the medicine of today. Magic was all that was left. This does not mean that healing did not occur. On the contrary, it may have occurred as often as, or more often than, today. 'Magic' is not necessarily an inferior mode of healing; it is just different. It is not based on 'reason', that is all.

Today the shaman appears to be an historical artifact. This may, in part, be because of the occultist nature of his wares. But too much emphasis on magic and ritual is misplaced. Pre-scientific medicine, as bizarre as it often appears, was also doggedly pragmatic. In many cases elegant rituals were premised on sound empirical observations. Lord Ritchie-Calder, quoting Oliver Wendell Holmes Sr, points out that early medicine appropriated 'everything from every source that can be of the slightest use to anybody who is ailing in any way . . .'[15]

At its root, the paradigm of early medicine – the shamanistic tradition – was based on 'balance'; man and Nature coexist in an uneasy equilibrium which must be restored before individual cures and community consensus can be achieved. Claude Levi-Strauss characterizes the paradigm this way:

> That the mythology of the shaman does not correspond to objective reality does not matter. The patient believes in it and belongs to a society that believes in it. The protecting spirits, the evil spirits, the supernatural monsters and magical monsters are elements of a coherent system which are the basis of the natives' concept of the universe. The patient accepts them, or rather she has never doubted them. What she does not accept are the incomprehensible and arbitrary pains which represent an element foreign to her system but which the shaman, by invoking the myth, will replace in a whole in which everything has its proper place.[16]

From Shaman to Doctor

To the shaman, a person was an organism in vital inter-action with other living things and, in some cases, with inanimate matter as well. Thus the shaman's approach to healing was necessarily holistic. The person alone was not the problem – disease was not just the inhabitant of a corporeal shell. Moreover, the person was not just a body; it was impossible to work with the body alone. The context was too important.

The Cartesian thesis that mind and matter were divisible drove a wedge between the mind and the body that persists in Western medicine today. Descartes's assertion shattered the notion that man could be viewed holistically. The split has been slowly healing, but the cure is far away for medicine. As William Irwin Thompson says:

> . . . [I]n our physical sciences we have long since gone beyond the 18th century notion of dead hunks of matter moving in the black void of space. Yet, our psychological sciences are still restricted to 18th century mechanistic notions: minds are simply . . . hunks of grey matter moving in the black void of time.[17]

This is true of the health sciences as well. A doctor, well versed in intellectual history, may comprehend the antiquarian nature of the division of mind and matter, but in his practice he will nevertheless isolate the body as a machine in need of repair.

The Cartesian division of mind and body may be a shibboleth. But as a way of looking at the world, it was seized by medical science as a way of organizing its endeavour. Following this bias, medicine has become the most rigidly mechanistic of the sciences. In *The Natural Mind,* Andrew Weil characterizes medicine's preoccupation with material reality this way:

> Modern allopathic medicine is essentially materialistic. For example, the widely accepted germ theory of disease – a cornerstone of allopathic theory – states that certain microscopic entities (bacteria and viruses are the most important) whose appearance in space and time correlates well with other physical manifestations of illness are causative of illness.[18]

In contrast, Weil stresses the importance of the 'unconscious', or the mind, in achieving health. Whether Weil is right or not in his assumptions about health, his diagnosis of modern medicine's perceptions of reality is accurate.

Prior to Descartes, medicine was a compound of magic and empirics. It relied on magical formulations, and also upon techniques consistent with observations of man and Nature indigenous to a given tribe or culture. But with the body freed of the larger man, and conceptualized as a machine, medicine at least had a manageable subject – the metaphor of the body as a machine. The shaman was a pivotal cultural figure who utilized both healing techniques and communal ceremony. But a shaman was not needed to tinker with a machine; what was needed was a mechanic. The class of shamans could now be replaced by the class of mechanics.

The metaphor of man as a machine is probably overworked. But it is central to an understanding of the rise of the class of doctors. And the idea of the body as a machine to the biologist is highly explanatory. However, in medicine's hands it was perverted in practice. To think of man as a machine does aid us in understanding something about bodily function, but it does not follow that treating the body as a machine will heal it. Thomas McKeown, an expert on the period, sums it up this way:

> The approach to biology and medicine established during the seventeenth century was an engineering one based on a physical model. Nature was conceived in mechanistic terms, which lead in biology to the idea that a living organism could be regarded as a machine which might be taken apart and reassembled if its structure and function were fully understood. In medicine, the same concept leads further to the belief that an understanding of disease processes and of the body's response to them would make it possible to intervene therapeutically, mainly by physical (surgical), chemical, or electrical methods.[19]

The emerging medical technologies, though unsophisticated, matched the machine metaphor. Blood-letting persisted, cauterization was used and purgatives were also common. But medicine remained outside the body – at least until it was clear that the body could not be understood without an examination of its inner workings, just as a car's engine cannot be repaired without looking under the bonnet. The first anatomy textbook was published by Vesralius in 1543. But about two hundred years passed before the investigation of what went on inside the skin was widely tolerated.

The image of the body as a machine had been planted, but despite its power the era was transitional. The technology was residual. Anachronisms like treatments based on bodily humours remained. But it was also the 'age of the eye', as the Renaissance has been called. It was now expected that knowledge would be a compilation of observations rather than an endless elaboration of theological propositions. Until the publication of Virchow's *Cellular Pathology*[20] in 1858, medicine moved alternatively through old wisdom and new findings. The doctor had emerged, but a theoretical framework for medicine had not.

The Era of Public Health

Today there are two ways to deliver health. The first is through industrialized services and the second is through systemic measures designed to create threshold conditions for health. The latter, public health, is starved of resources but is still recognized as essential to well-being – without potable water, for instance, disease is inevitable. But it was not always so.

It has long been acknowledged that there was some sort of link between disease and the environment. Bur prior to the emergence of the germ theory of disease, the link was more spiritual than physical. In this sense the shaman was the first public health practitioner. The shaman might direct that a house contaminated by the illness of a resident be burned. Although it is possible that the measure was grounded in physical observation, its larger utility may have been symbolic. In any event, these early measures, while conceptually consistent with public health, are modest compared to the measures which characterized the nineteenth century. As early as 1853, John Snow, a London physician, linked a cholera epidemic to contaminated water in a public water-pump. But it took the genius of Pasteur, Koch and others, later in the century, to tie infectious disease to environmental sources.

Today it is common knowledge that air, water and solid waste contain disease agents. But late in the nineteenth century the idea was revolutionary. The perception of man as a machine persisted. But the breakthroughs of Pasteur and others modified the metaphor. Man was still a machine, and disease a malfunction, but with new information about the impact of the environment it became clear that machine malfunctions could be introduced by virulent agents in the environment.

And the results were much better. Medicine had slowly improved, but the health of the population remained roughly the same. Maternal and infant mortality rates held constant, and longevity was not significantly lengthened. The introduction of public health programmes radically altered the picture. Pettenkofer demonstrated that the installation of sanitary sewage systems in Munich led to immediate improvements in health status.[21] And there were other breakthroughs. In 1812, the death rate for tuberculosis in New York was 700 per 10,000. Seventy years later, after the first bacillus had been cultured by Koch, the rate had dropped to 400. By 1910 it was down to 180, and by 1945 or so, before antibiotics became widely used, the rate had reached 48. These clear and unmistakable results inevitably influenced the public's conception of health. No longer was health the result of caprice, occasionally aided by the physician. Now it was possible to create environmental conditions which enhanced the opportunities for health.

The technologies of public health were different. The old technologies of personal medicine were steadily becoming more refined – ultimately to reach a state of high refinement, even mannerism. But the implementation of public health programmes required more complex tools. For example, improvements in the quality of water were dependent on knowledge of chemical interaction, but in order to implement the programmes political negotiation was also required. And then the public had to be convinced. But once the gains in health were clear, public health – or population medicine – joined the physician in the pursuit of health. This necessarily forced a reconceptualization of health:

> Concern for the quality of the environment achieved a rational and coherent expression during the second half of the nineteenth century. In Western Europe and then in the United States, the early phases of the Industrial Revolution had resulted in crowding, misery, accumulation of filth, horrible working and living conditions, ugliness in all the mushrooming industrial areas, and high rates of sickness and mortality everywhere. The physical and mental decadence of the working classes became intolerable to the social conscience and in addition constituted a threat to the future of industrial civilization.
> ... Our nineteenth-century forebears approached their problems through a creative philosophy of man in his environment.[22]

Despite its successes public health, like personal health, could be carried to illogical extremes. Health, like disease, is the result of many factors. Perhaps the greatest debt we owe to René Dubos lies in his recognition that the cause of disease is multiple. For decades (and even in some backwaters still today) it was assumed that disease was caused by a 'single bullet', a single cause. This is the premise of the germ theory of disease, patiently constructed by such pioneers as Pasteur, Koch and Lister.[23] The germ theory of disease emerged from the new knowledge yielded by public health programming. Earlier cultures were aware of the potentially debilitating impact of the environment, but they had no specific theory of causation. But with the knowledge that water, air, sewage and other matter contained 'germs', even though they could not always be 'seen', the germ theory of disease evolved. Countless investigators pursued the identification of as many 'germs' as possible. Soon the assumption emerged that a given disease had a given cause – a specific agent or 'germ'. This theory permeated medical practice and is implicit in much of medical care today. But, as Dubos and others have argued, there is much more to the theory. Dubos, for example, acknowledges that there is a 'physiological' basis to disease – that there are disease agents – but he convincingly accounts for the greater impact of environmental and social factors. In simple terms, every person carries the 'potential' for every disease at all times. But through circumstances which vary with every individual, some people get sick while others, similarly situated, do not. This is not the same thing as saying that disease has no 'physical' base, but rather that the physical base for disease, which probably varies with the nature of the disease, must be 'triggered' by events external to the individual. A logical extension of this theory is that some people 'select' diseases (or injuries) because they find illness preferable to stress.[24] This is exemplified by the work of some sociologists, notably Talcott Parsons, on 'sick roles'. Parsons and others believe that some individuals choose, or are forced to choose, to play a sick role in given social settings.[25]

The paradigm of medicine was not modified as much as augmented by the rise of public health – the practice of medical care remained largely static. Doctors continued to tinker with the human machine, paying less and less attention to the larger setting in which the machine functioned. But the introduction of public health measures necessarily engendered a sense of health as an ecological concept – it was necessary for man to understand the delicate balance between the species and the environment in order to achieve health. The concept was not wholly new. It was, and is, a fundamental proposition of Christian theology that the earth should serve the ends of man. The theories of public health fit that dominant view.

This recognition has remained peripheral to medicine. The successes of public health became a part of common wisdom, but the fundamental paradigm of medical practice was only slightly enriched – it was not altered. The engineering approach remained dominant. The environment was amenable to engineering as the human body was to doctoring. The activities were complementary. Both the body and the environment could be treated by mechanics. There could be both patient medicine and population medicine. The marriage lasted until the early twentieth century.

The Science of Services

Medicine yielded to the 'logic' of the scientific method as it passed into this century. Lawrence Henderson, a physician, made a frequently-used observation that 'somewhere between 1910 and 1912 in this country, a random patient, with a random disease, consulting a doctor chosen at random had, for the first time in the history of mankind, a better than fifty-fifty chance of profiting from the encounter.'[26] Just over a hundred years ago, only one-half of the children born in the United States reached fifty. And until fifty years ago there were few effective therapies. Care consisted largely of prolonged nursing home stays and the alleviation of those symptoms amenable to the few weapons medicine possessed. Hospitals were virtually unknown until the late nineteenth century. Medicine simply did not have enough technology to house in specialized facilities. Hospitals were not needed until medicine became mass-produced, until convenience to the doctor became more important than the welfare of the patient. The early practitioner could manage his patients with bedside manners, a few nostrums, some salves and balms, and a few tools.*

Introduction of the scientific method to medicine has resulted in indisputable benefits. But one of the casualties has been public health. The division between medicine and public health occurred early in this century, at about the time that medicine became infatuated with the scientific method. Kerr White, a medical care researcher at Johns Hopkins University, refers to the early twentieth-century division of medicine and public health this way:

> The drive to improve medicine cure to the neglect of medicine care carried the day. Flexner's views prevailed and the 'basic' sciences of medical education were declared to be biochemistry and physiology; the equally 'fundamental' sciences of epidemiology, economics and sociology were excluded from the curriculum. In spite of the pathologist Virchow's admonition that medicine is essentially a social science, America opted for individual medicine largely to the exclusion of population medicine ... Population medicine was relegated to so-called schools of public health after World War I.[27]

Although public health was a casualty of the science of medicine, the machine metaphor was not – if anything it was strengthened. The machine was simply recognized as more complex. And there were a few new ideas. One that contributed to the view of the world which guided medicine was 'repeatability' – a specific intervention would produce the same result in every patient (controlling for a few individual differences, including age, fitness, etc.). The results of medical care, then, were not idiosyncratic – there were patterns which could be predicted and laws which could be derived because

---

* The churches were first responsible for hospital construction, but more as a haven for the homeless than a place for the provision of care. My reference is to the 'modern' hospital, focused on the provision of care for the sick. For a general history of hospitals, see Mary Risley, *House of Healing: The Story of the Hospital* (Doubleday, New York, 1961).

the results of care logically followed from the intervention. The hypothesis was the diagnosis, the 'experiment' was the intervention and the cure the confirmation. Medicine had once again left the world of magic. And, if this was so, refinement of technique became critical. If the results of care were dependent on specific interventions, then the more precision of technique there was the more accurate would be the prediction and the more repeatable the results.

The technologies of 'scientific' medicine were largely aimed at reducing the tolerance for error. The patient was a machine and would necessarily respond to carefully programmed interventions. Hence, the hospital was necessary to immobilize the patient in need of the more radical interventions, featuring surgery and chemotherapy. If patients could be placed in a homogenous environment, fewer variables could influence the result. But because the physician could still influence the result if he modified the rules of the game, technicians were needed and artists were unwelcome. In 1910, as a result of the Flexner Report, the number of medical schools in the United States was reduced to leave only those most capable of turning out technicians. If repeatability was important, there were concomitants. The specific problem or disease had to be accurately classified so as to permit application of those processes designed to cure the condition. Measurement was integral to technical medicine. In the eighteenth century physicians were fascinated by the taxonomy of disease. In the nineteenth century it became an obsession. The classification of diseases was central to the success of a scientific medicine. Disease conditions had to be placed into categories so that appropriate techniques could be utilized according to the category into which the patient was placed.

Medicine now had a product - what it lacked was a marketing system. Prior to the twentieth century, patients pursued cures. But now that health could be conceptualized as a commodity - a product that could be delivered over and over again - a 'delivery system' was needed to facilitate distribution. A 'need' was perceived - patients with specific diseases. A product was conceptualized to meet the need - medical care services (that is, surgery, drugs, diagnostic tools, etc.). Distribution could be handled through hospitals and physicians' offices. And finally, marketing and promotion would be entrusted to insurance companies, largely controlled by physicians, and to the government, which was under increasing pressure to assume the costs of care.

Once again, despite the surge of new technology, the paradigm of medicine was only subtly altered. At its roots it remained constant. Disease was still a functional disorder in a machine for which machine-tooled parts were needed. But as the business of medicine became more precise, and as medical techniques evolved, their delivery could be systematized. Disease was not an idiosyncratic reaction. Disease was a malfunction in the human machine, either through an internal disorder or through the activity of an external agent. The most effective way to treat disease was first to accurately classify it, and then to apply a like set of techniques designed to produce a like cure in like patients. Since the services did not have to be individualized, a delivery system was created. Health was now essentially a fungible commodity like salt or sugar. Medicine then became almost entirely disease-oriented, because it was disease that it could classify and treat. Technical medicine ascended, and the arts of medicine withered. Medicine was close to being synonymous with health.

Medicine, A.D. 1975

Today there are about 45,000 physicians in the National Health Service in Great Britain. And there are nearly 300,000 practising physicians in the United States. There are over 7,000 hospitals in the United States and about 3,200 in Great Britain. And in each country physicians and hospitals are served by a vast and profitable supply system, of which the pharmaceuticals are the most pervasive and profitable. Medical care has become a very big business – even if, as in Great Britain, it appears in the guise of a public utility.

The public has, in its turn, become profoundly dependent on medicine. It searches for cures that do not exist, and, with the exception of a few, it fails to seek health in other ways. The public has been persuaded that health is a function of medical care – medical care has become synonymous with health.

This thinking is relatively new. Prior to this century, even prior to the nineteen-twenties, patients had to initiate contact with the medical care system and to pay for whatever they got. There was virtually no public pressure for change because the benefits of medical care were marginal, and the public did not highly value it. Antibiotics had not been discovered, and surgical and diagnostic techniques were crude. The improvements in health status that had been achieved were due to public health measures, not medicine. But in the two decades that followed, medicine was the beneficiary of new technologies. Penicillin was discovered in 1928, and the other antibiotics soon followed. Still more and better physicians were trained, in part due to the aftermath of the Flexner Report. These changes had a predictable impact on the public's perception of medicine – as medical care became more effective, more people perceived its benefits. But although the public's perceptions had changed, medicine had not. Disease is still presumed to be the result of faulty machinery. And because all machines were roughly the same, treatments could be finely tuned to fit discrete diagnoses. But today's medicine has driven the metaphor of the machine to extremes. Specialization now translates into superspecialization. No longer is the specialist content to deal with a bodily system, such as the neurological system; it is now possible to specialize in plastic repair of the eye orbit.

The medical delivery system has also become highly elaborated – so much so that the average patient is often completely confused. But most significant has been the further conceptualization of the patient as a machine of great complexity. In the past, the physician may have thought of his patient as a machine, but nevertheless had to treat him as a whole machine. Today, with the exception of a few hardy rural practitioners and family physicians, medicine has compartmentalized the body into finer and finer machine parts. It is one thing to treat a patient as a machine, ignoring rich information related to health and functioning, but it is another to subdivide the body into its constituent parts. In the former medicine, at least the possibility existed for holistic treatment. In today's medicine this is impossible. Medicine focuses on the smallest 'bits' of material reality – symptoms – and ignores a buzzing profusion of phenomena which may be related to health.

The technologies of today's medicine match its preoccupation with disease in the constituent parts of the human machine. Surgery has become more prevalent and more profound. Drugs flow nearly unimpeded from doctor to patient; often for conditions like viral disorders, for which there is no chemical cure. The delivery system has become large, unwieldly and complex – an industry in search of newer and more refined products. Today's medicine has succeeded where the medicines of the past have failed: it has equated medical care with health. But the borders of the prevailing paradigm are blurring. It is becoming increasingly clear that health is not the same as medicine – that the wrong questions have deservedly received the wrong answers. A new paradigm for health is slowly emerging.

A New Medicine

All other species work within the existing habitat. Their success or failure depends upon their ability to adapt to the conditions in which they find themselves. Their survival depends upon a complex, interrelated ecosystem of which they form a small part and over which they have very limited control ...

Man alone has tried to deny his relationship to the total ecosystem of which he forms part by continuously ignoring and cutting off feedback which he finds undesirable. He has developed the habit of seeing his habitat as totally flexible according to his own wishes and desires.[28]

The history of health has been the history of adaptation. Through adaptation, not medical care, man has achieved improved health. The environmental insults of the industrial age – contaminated water and lack of sanitation, the unavailability of basic nutrients, uncontrolled epidemics, famine and an inadequate understanding of infectious transmission – have been brought under control. But the environmental insults of today have not. The contribution of medical care was marginal in the adaptation of man to industrial threats; similarly, it has only a minor role to play in the adaptations that now face us. The reason for this lies in the paradigm of health that medicine has conceived:'. . . To find out how an organism works by taking it to pieces and trying to put it together again from knowledge of the parts.'[29] Medicine has ignored the understanding of man that is implicit in our evolutionary history. It has sought to engineer human health through the manipulation of human parts. John Powles, Professor of Anthropology at the University of Sussex, puts the point this way in his paper 'On the Limitations of Modern Medicine':

> The engineering approach to the improvement of health has been dominant over an alternative approach which would emphasize the importance of way of life factors in disease – an approach which could be described as "ecological." While it is to changes with which this latter approach is concerned that industrial man largely owes his current standard of health, it is in the engineering approach that he has placed his faith. Curative medicine has not been very successful in reducing the impact of diseases of maladaptation.[30]

As a population, particularly in the more developed world, we face adaptation problems for which medicine is not equipped. But we do not have all the pieces in place for a new medicine – in fact, we do not even know what all the pieces are. We know that something different is needed. And we know that it is in the relationship between man and his environment that the key to health lies. Health is not just the well-oiled functioning of the body – it is achieved through the strategic collaboration of man with his world, expressed through a series of 'relationships'. These include the relationships between mind and matter, man and Nature, man and the social roles he plays, and man and higher consciousness, even spirituality. Physicians can help, but the individual is ultimately responsible for the quality of those relationships. It is the individual who must re-establish harmonious relationships with his environment. This may sound utopian, but it is historically sound – it is the way we sought health before we had modern medicine.

In the essays that follow some of the 'elements' of a 'new science' and, in turn, a new medicine can be perceived. Some of the essays offer some concrete suggestions; others only scatter inferences; still others leave all the work up to the reader. Consequently, short 'bridging' sections link the essays to one another. Then, in a short concluding chapter, a few more strands are pulled together.

CHAPTER III

A New Medicine:
Emerging Concepts and Research

The medicine of today will soon become the old medicine. It stresses the isolation of the individual whose health is largely, if not entirely, a function of his environment. Some health has been the result. But health for the future, a future presenting the species with new challenges of adaptation, will require new concepts and new initiatives. A new medicine will be organized around a number of new concepts. Four of these emerging concepts were featured in discussions at the May Lectures:

1. The complex interrelationship between mind and body – that is, the voluntary control of internal states and a fuller development of 'psychosomatic' medicine.
2. The interconnectedness of the human species with Nature, as it embraces other living things, environmental factors such as light and sound, social conditions such as pace and congestion, and energy functions, such as electronic pollution, which is mostly ill-understood.
3. 'Communications' between and among living things and systems – that is, telepathic communications and electromagnetic field effects.
4. A deeper understanding of the dynamics of healing, with emphasis on the multi-faceted 'causes' of disease – that is, the patient's susceptibilities, needs and motivations, and the role of the healer, both technically and anthropologically.

The medicine of the future will be characterized by the comprehension and articulation of a series of 'relationships' between the patient and everything around that patient, including the doctor. Today health is defined as the absence of disease. Tomorrow health will be defined as a symbiotic and balanced relationship between the person and his or her environment.

In the essays that follow many of these new 'elements', or strands, of an emerging medicine are discussed. The pieces by Elmer Green and the Simontons focus on the mind-body interaction. Lyall Watson and E. Stanton Maxey, in very different ways, look at the interconnectedness question. Communications between or among living systems are taken up in one particular respect – plant research – by both Cleve Backster and Marcel Vogel. Finally, Norman Shealy and Sister Justa Smith examine the healing process.

There are three 'unclassifiable' presentations. It is tempting to classify Andrija Puharich's presentation as an example of 'communication', and in some respects that would be appropriate. But because it raises such profoundly different possibilities, it is treated separately.

For different reasons, the essay by Werner Erhard is also hard to classify. At one level it is an example of 'interconnectedness'. Erhard bears down hard on the form and substance of 'reality' in an attempt to convince the listener that 'attachment' to the immovable object and the irresistible force is foolish and wasteful. The essay has obvious implications for health, principally mental health as we arbitrarily classify our lack of well-being. But again, because it does not fit easily into one of the four concepts, it is presented separately.

Finally there is David Tansley's essay. Tansley is essentially interested in the more intangible and spiritual aspects of the human condition. In this context he argues that health and disease cannot be fully understood unless those aspects of human nature, and their impact on the physical body, are more fully understood. Much of what Tansley had to say was difficult to comprehend by those who were unfamiliar with his conceptual terrain. Yet his perspective added a dimension to the discussion that it would otherwise have lacked. Moreover, one of the cultural transformations now becoming visible is a reawakening of spiritual interest. Movements such as Arica and Hare Krishna, found more widely in the United States than in Great Britain, and spiritual centres such as the Divine Light Mission (led by Sat Sun Maraji Ji) and Naropa University are evidence. Thus while Tansley's concepts, and even terminology, are foreign to many, they share some common and expanding ground.

The essays vary in style and trenchancy. But, of course, this is true of essays about today's medicine as well. Hence, given that we do not know very much about health, all the essays have been included in one form or another; some have been simply excerpted.

The Relationships between Mind and Body

With the fresh understanding that the mind and the body are not incommensurable, research on mind-body interactions has flourished in recent years. One of the most promising fields of research is biofeedback – the technique of learning the voluntary control of internal states. The research is variegated, but some fundamental principles have emerged. First, it is possible for people to 'regulate' psychological states formerly thought to be involuntary. These include body temperature, heartbeat rate, brain wave rate, and perhaps even mood and emotion. Second, the skill is not necessarily differentially distributed in the population – it appears that nearly everyone can achieve some competence. Third, there appear to be some potentially powerful applications for health and healing, including control of headaches and hypertension. Fourth, and finally, there is little consensus on 'how' the subject exercises the control – at first biofeedback machines must be used, but soon most subjects can achieve control of some processes without using the equipment.

Many investigators have entered the field, and articles and books on the subject are appearing everywhere.[1] But there is near consensus on one proposition: Elmer Green is the 'dean' of biofeedback research. In the essay which follows, he outlines the field in general terms and then adds some speculations about the evolution of biofeedback practice.

BIOFEEDBACK AND VOLUNTARY CONTROL OF
INTERNAL STATES

Elmer Green, Ph.D.

What is Biofeedback?

The thread that will be running through the whole of my talk is that of volition: what human beings can do, can 'will' to do, with the insides of their bodies – at the level of the individual cell, or at the level of body systems, like the circulatory system for example. I will refer to some of the unusual people that we have worked with in our laboratory in Topeka, and also talk about our trip to India in search of yogis.

Stories of the feats of yogis have been coming out of India for the past two or three hundred years. Though these stories have been scoffed at, they have refused to die. Finally people have begun to wonder if there might be something to the stories after all. One source of interest has been the growing attention paid to hypnosis by the medical profession during the last century. If people could perform remarkable feats under hypnosis, perhaps the yogis, through some form of self-hypnosis, could do so as well.

In Germany, about 1910, Johannes Schultz started a programme which he called autogenic training – meaning self-generated or self-motivated training. He had been interested in yoga and hypnotism, but abandoned the latter about the same time as Freud, on the grounds that hypnosis was so idiosyncratic; its results were not sufficiently repeatable. The patients' resistance was often the reason. As a result, Schultz wondered if control over the process could be given to the patient himself. If the patient were giving himself instructions, maybe his resistance to them would dissipate. He would, for instance, get a patient to say to himself such phrases as 'I feel quite quiet,' while at the same time allowing himself to be quiet. This approach works. You can say to yourself, 'My hands are warm,' and in a while they will feel, and actually be, warmer.

We, that is my wife and I, began our work in 1964. We

attended the Menninger Foundation autogenic training programme in 1964. Most of the physicians attending the programme had never heard of autogenic training. But my wife and I decided to investigate what a person could do to change their physiological states. We began with some women. We wired them up in a psychophysiological laboratory to equipment that monitored the bodily processes we wished to examine. The purpose was to determine the extent to which, if at all, individuals could regulate some 'internal' functions.

We trained thirty-three women for two weeks in a programme of relaxation and hand-warming. Eventually, several could raise the temperature of their hands between two and ten degrees Fahrenheit. Encouraged, we decided to add biofeedback to the programme. Up to this point, only my wife and I had studied the equipment read-outs; the trainees did not see them. But biofeedback requires the individual to receive direct and continuous information about his or her performance. So we turned our monitors around so that the trainees could see what was happening. The result was that people who were given biofeedback in the course of autogenic training learned much faster. The programme was now a programme of self-regulation. At the time we did not understand how, if you told your hands to get warm, they got warm. Even today, we do not have a complete understanding. For example, an epileptic learns to discourage the type of brain rhythms likely to lead to an epileptic seizure – but we do not fully understand the process by which this takes place. How does a person select a brain pattern?

The figure on page 50 (Figure 1) divides the nervous system into two sections. These I label 'conscious' and 'unconscious'. (Psychological terms can be avoided by using the labels 'voluntary nervous system' and 'involuntary nervous system'.) Information usually comes to us through our external senses – sight, smell, sound, etc. This information might be called OUTS – outside-the-skin information. External information usually arouses an emotional response in us, but the response is not always obvious or even consciously accessible. We know that there is a system deep in the brain, the limbic

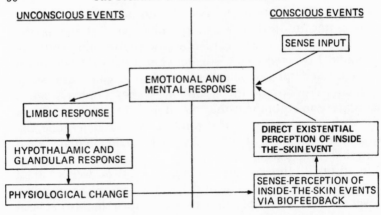

FIG. 1

system, which registers whenever emotional excitement is felt. This has been determined by the use of electrode implants. The reverse is also the case. If we stimulate the limbic system, conscious excitement is experienced.

The limbic system is connected with the hypothalamus. This small organ, in turn, is connected with (and regulates) the visceral and glandular systems of the body – the smooth muscles, the intestines, etc. None of this is news; it has been well known for some time that external information entering the organism is filtered through levels of the nervous system where it ultimately produces appropriate bodily reactions and changes. What *is* new is this: we now know that information arising from inside the organism (of which the individual may be completely unaware consciously) when displayed on monitoring meters and then fed into the brain, in the same way in which any external (OUTS) information passes to the brain, can cause the same organismic response – it can produce internal changes. The result is a cybernetic loop. Inside-the-skin information, INTS, is converted to outside-the-skin information, OUTS. This OUTS information is then fed back into the system, leading to or producing new INTS, which is then once again externalized. And so the loop is continued.

Putting it simply and non-technically, all that we apparently need to do to learn voluntary control of a physiological function, that is normally unconscious, is to acquire some information about it that we can consciously understand.

The equipment we use to display bodily states is not always needed. After people have worked with a biofeedback device for a while, they cease to need it. Somehow the subject learns how to consciously perceive unconscious states. The cybernetic loop looses a link. The subject can directly control inside-the-skin events. A cardiac patient in Baltimore, for example, initially learned to control her rate of heartbeat through a biofeedback monitoring device. She reduced her heart rate from 110 to 60/70 beats per minute over a period of three months. During that time she discovered that she no longer required the machine. Consequently, the difference between biofeedback and yoga may not be great. Yoga is harder and takes longer to master, perhaps because the adept must work on a kind of hit-or-miss basis; only marginal physiological cues are available. Only as the yogi succeeds in acquiring some control – that is, actually manages to produce larger changes within himself – can he then become rapidly more adept, because he now has an adequate flow of information.

In our laboratory we have constructed a biofeedback device that makes it possible for people to learn to control a number of physiological variables simultaneously. One rising bar in the display panel might represent muscle relaxation, another heart rate, a third galvanic skin potential, a fourth hand temperature and so on. The nearer the bar rises to the top of the display in each case, the more 'control' the subject demonstrates.

One of the most frequent applications of biofeedback technology focuses on brainwave frequencies. Alpha and the other brain rhythms were discovered about 1935 by Berger. He placed an electrode on the back of a subject's head and picked up an electrical rhythm of about ten cycles per second. This was the first frequency he observed and that is probably why he called it alpha. The second type of frequency – beta waves – appeared when the alpha rhythm disappeared. Alpha waves vary between eight and thirteen cycles per second. They occur in about ninety per cent of the population whenever the eyes are closed and thinking is random. The beta wave frequency is about thirteen to twenty-five cycles per second. Both rhythms occur when the eyes are open and attention is focused. It is possible to produce alpha waves with the eyes open – if you are sitting staring into the distance, or are trapped in a boring conversation in which your attention is wandering, then you will probably produce alpha rhythms. Through the use of biofeedback, a subject can 'learn' to generate a certain brain rhythm, although theta and delta rhythms, both of which are lower in frequency and are associated with sleep or semi-conscious states, are more difficult to produce.

Some Uses of Biofeedback

Among the possibilities for the use of biofeedback is the control of migraine headaches and related conditions. Headaches are probably related to high levels of tension and, to some degree, to a restricted flow of blood through the brain or scalp. Tension and the flow of blood are generally considered functions of the autonomic system. Accordingly, in principle, control can be learned through biofeedback.*

How we learn to control, and what the physiological processes are that are induced, is uncertain. It is possible, however, to be slightly more precise about the probable mechanics of migraine and its relief. People who suffer from migraine usually have abnormally cold hands. They can learn to warm up their hands through biofeedback, like other people, but in this case the increase achieved is as much as twenty-five degrees Fahrenheit. Improving the flow of blood in the hands – making them warm – often results in elimination of the migraine. This is a matter of simple hydraulics; the result is not achieved by drawing the blood away from the brain and the scalp. Soaking the subject's hands in hot water, which also makes them warm, has no effect on the headache in the majority of cases. What appears to happen in biofeedback is that in learning to control the flow of blood in the hands, the patient is learning both how to relax and how to engage the entire autonomic nervous

* The absence of alpha waves is one index of tension. Mental patients are often unable to produce them, or if they can, do so only sporadically. Learning to produce them is closely associated with learning how to relax.

system in the blood flow process. The benefits of improving blood flow in one part of the body are then generalized (by the central hypothalamic control) to all parts of the system, including the head. The loss of the migraine appears to be a fortunate by-product.

Our interests, however, are not limited to the physiological aspects of psychosomatic illness and disturbance. We are also interested in psychological processes. For example, we have done a substantial amount of research on theta brain waves. The theta wave is an even slower rhythm than alpha, from four to six cycles per second. It begins usually just before we actually fall asleep, when we are very quiet and still. If theta is produced without the individual actually falling asleep, although that is what usually occurs, then the subject experiences hypnagogic images. A hypnagogic image is one that flashes vividly and completely into the mind, often with considerable detail and complexity. Most of us experience this phenomenon briefly and occasionally at the edge of sleep. Biofeedback can be used to help trainees induce theta waves without succumbing to sleep. When this happens, the hypnagogic images become more plentiful and persist. They are not consciously created; they are self-generating.

Theta waves and the associated hypnagogic images are important from several points of view. For example, a number of eminent scientists and artists report in their auto-biographies that hypnagogic images were sometimes the source of their best ideas. Hypnagogic images in creative individuals may represent an aspect of their genius. Theta waves may be related to creativity.

We also found that the increased production of theta waves – as with alpha waves – produced greater well-being, better work output and more relaxed and convivial personal relationships in most subjects. These results were also experienced by mental patients. Some patients seem to get information from their unconscious in the form of hypnagogic images, which aids them and their psychiatrists in the resolution of their problems.

Swami Rama

The heart control experiment referred to above was only one

of a continuing series of experiments at the Menninger Foundation. The experiments were a part of the Menninger Voluntary Controls Programme. One day one of the doctors who had graduated from Menninger called me on the phone and said he had found a yogi who could make his pulse disappear. This seemed mildly interesting so we agreed that this yogi, Swami Rama, should come to the Foundation for a series of tests. When he arrived, we connected him to our monitoring devices. He then stated that initially he would differentiate the temperature in two spots on his hand; he said he would heat up one place and cool the other.

The results, briefly, were as follows. Over a five minute period the temperature of both spots drifted up slightly. Then there was a distinct shift in the record, and the temperature of both began to drop. But then the temperature below the little finger began to rise while that below the thumb went down and stayed down. We talked a little, and then the yogi said he was about to do something. At that point the temperature of both spots began to rise. Then the one below the thumb went down again while the other continued to rise. Finally, we had a difference of eleven degrees Fahrenheit between the two areas.

Then we did the heart experiment. On the cardiotachometer record his heart produced an initial rate of 66 beats per minute. Then it speeded up to almost 94 beats and finally dropped to 62. This fluctuation was interesting, but other subjects had achieved comparable results. Suddenly the yogi called out, 'What is my heart doing now?' At this point he had increased the 'dub' half of the normal 'flub-dub' beat, so that it was unusually large – something like 'flub-DUB, flub-DUB,' to represent this in words. When he did this, his rate shot up from around 66 to around 84 beats per minute. We then requested the Swami to slow down his heart rate. Quickly he reduced it from 70 beats per minute to around 52. The session ended.

The Swami was due to depart for Minneapolis the next day, but he was distressed that he had not 'stopped' his heart for us. Originally he had said that he needed to fast for three days before attempting to do so. This was logical if 'control' was to be achieved; it would be exercised through the vagus nerve, which also controls the stomach and a good deal of the viscera. Indigestion could result from interference with that nerve. Nevertheless, the Swami announced that he would make the attempt without fasting. He was interested to find out if there would be any side effects. And, second, he did not want to forgo the opportunity of being recorded. In any case, he said, his own teacher could stop his heart at any time without any preparation. So we agreed to the attempt. We did *not* agree, however, to the Swami's proposal that he would stop his heart for three to four minutes! Ten seconds would be enough for us.

The next day he performed. Our records reflect that his heart rate of 70 beats per minute suddenly rose to 300 beats per minute for a period of 17 seconds. At this point my wife in the control room called, 'That's all,' our pre-arranged signal to conclude the experiment. But we were puzzled – if his heart had stopped, why did our records show 300 beats per minute? We took the graph to a cardiologist for his opinion. He told us the 300 beats per minute signal was known as atrial flutter. This occurs when the heart is not pumping blood; the valves are not working and the chambers are not filling with blood. Blood pressure drops and the person faints. What, by the way, he asked us, had happened to this patient? We told him 'nothing' – the Swami just took off the electrodes and went out and gave a lecture.

The Swami's performance has considerable implications for those with irregular heart function. Many people experience involuntary flutter, though their problem is not how to turn it on, but how to turn it off or stop it. The Swami has shown us that it is possible to consciously affect the rate of heart beat. The use of biofeedback may aid sufferers.

A Trip to India, and a Trip With Jack Schwartz

Swami Rama also told us that there were other interesting people in India we should meet. A year later we organized an expedition to the subcontinent. We tested seventeen individuals, among them three of four yogis (subjects who could extensively control the physiological functions). One yogi could make his heart miss beats. Another stayed in an airtight box for 7½ hours, producing continuous alpha rhythms, and without enough air.

Another yogi had apparently learned to 'control' the pain response through sitting on nails. He lived on the banks of the Ganges and weighed only ninety pounds. He lived from people's charity and had taken a vow of silence; he had not spoken for twelve years. (In the taxi he instructed the driver where to go, but no matter; he *could* control his pain reactions – we have records to demonstrate it.) We still have not fully analyzed the data we collected in India. One of the reasons is that we discovered someone in the United States who could perform comparable feats.

I had heard about Jack Schwartz and invited him to come to the laboratory. About a year after the invitation was issued, he called and said he would come to the laboratory for eight days. When I looked in my diary all the days on either side of those dates were full, but the eight days were available.

We wired him up in the usual way. I had not known in advance what he would demonstrate. What he did was drive knitting needles through his biceps, without any expression of pain and (except as described below) without bleeding. Later he performed the same thing before an audience of fifty doctors. But before he began, he dropped the knitting needle on the floor and rubbed it along the floor with his shoe. In answer to our curious looks, he explained that he was sterilizing his equipment. Playing the 'straight man', I asked why he had never developed an infection. He replied roughly, 'All the cellular material of the body can be controlled by the mind. Normally we cannot do it because we are unaware or unconscious. Yet such functions are under the mind's control, and if I give instructions for my body not to interact with any foreign materials, how can I get an infection?'

By the time he had the needle buried about half an inch deep in his arm, I began to think that even if he did this a hundred times, I still would not believe that he could control his blood flow. Maybe, I thought, he has a peculiar skin. Consequently, with the intention of interfering with his concentration, I asked him if he would bleed when he pulled the needle out. I was thinking that I could interrupt his conscious-unconscious harmony. He looked startled and said that he did not think he would bleed. But when he took the needle out he did bleed, quite a lot in fact. We were mopping the blood up when he said in a soft voice, 'Now it stops.' Then, while I was actually looking at the puncture wound with the blood running out, it closed up in about one second. I congratulated him. We now knew that he could bleed like a normal person, but could also stop the bleeding at will. I suggested that he might like to do the whole thing again without bleeding. A long pause ensued, and I began to wonder what I had said wrong. Finally he said okay, and inserted the needle a second time in a slightly different place. This time the holes closed up quickly. There was no sub-dermal bleeding and there were no marks of any kind. All traces of one puncture had disappeared in twenty-four hours, and of the other three in seventy-two hours.

Later I asked Jack why he had paused before agreeing to a second trial. He explained that he would never 'force' his body to do anything. Instead, he had to request his body to perform the task – that is, he had to 'ask' his 'subconscious' if it was willing to co-operate. He also said that he had to clear the request with his 'paraconscious'. (Paraconscious is apparently his term for some kind of superconscious.) In other words, he is not willing to do 'tricks'. Apparently, he needs to feel that the effort is worthwhile. He apparently must seek confirmation, first from his subconscious and then from his paraconscious.

Swami Rama had discussed the same issue with us. His concern about stopping his heart for too long without having fasted stemmed from his fear of damaging his 'subtle heart'. He explained that the visible, physical organ which we see with our normal eyes is only a 'part' of a larger, invisible 'energy structure'. According to the Swami, this energy structure consists of several different parts. The physical organ – anatomically – is simply the 'densest' part of the structure. As he put it, 'All of the body is in the mind, but not all of the mind is in the body.' Every piece or cell of the body is in the mind. And all the cells can be controlled with the mind, once you are aware of them (see the essay by

David Tansley on this point).

The Swami also said that there were ten energies involved in the internal functioning of the body. He was able to control these energies – which he referred to as 'pranas'. Each prana relates to a chain of organs. What he described appeared to be consistent with acupuncture patterns, in particular the meridians.

The Swami's comments suggest that there is some kind of field or fields associated with the body. The Swami went further – he argued that there is a 'field of mind' surrounding the planet. There are a lot of 'pranas' or energies outside the skin, as well as the ten within it.

If this is so, then the work of Cleve Backster and others may be related – there may be meridians, or a medium of 'communication', lying in the spaces between tangible structures.

Theoretically, biofeedback holds enormous potential for self-healing. But there may also be some real limits to the control capacity of many, if not all, subjects. Then too there is the argument that biofeedback may be potentially harmful, even if apparently effective. Lewis Thomas, M.D., takes essentially this position when he argues that the problem is:

> If I was informed tomorrow that I was in direct communication with my liver and I could now take over, I would become deeply depressed. For I am, to face the facts squarely, considerably less intelligent than my liver. I am, moreover, constitutionally unable to make hepatic decisions, and I prefer not to be obliged to do so; I would not be able to think of the first thing to do.[2]

There are probably limits to the applications of biofeedback; this is likely to prove the case as the phenomenon is further researched. One of the disease conditions few have thought to be amenable to any kind of conscious control, limits notwithstanding, is cancer. Yet Carl and Stephanie Simonton have introduced the 'mind' into their practice. Carl, a physician, is a radiation therapist. Stephanie is a psychologist and works closely with Carl's patients, principally in a counselling role. Their use of meditation – or as they call it, 'relaxation and mental imagery' – as a therapeutic agent is integrated into a more conventional practice. Yet the fact that the meditation appears to be instrumental in the treatment is not altogether surprising. There is a small body of research which links meditation with changes in psychology and function. These include more efficient respiration, less stress, diminished use of drugs, alcohol and stimulants, and so on.[3] The Simontons' technique is disarmingly simple. Simonton first teaches his patients how to meditate and then instructs them about their disease process and the means by which the body's natural immunities resist the cancer. He then asks them to meditate on the disease process and the 'attack' on the disease by the immune system. It sounds simplistic and perhaps it is; but, according to Simonton, for those patients who use meditation the prognosis is roughly twice as favourable as another patient population matched for demographics, severity of disease and attitude.

THE ROLE OF THE MIND IN CANCER THERAPY

Carl Simonton, M.D. and Stephanie Simonton

The subject matter presented here is controversial. My subject is the role which the mind plays in the cause and cure of cancer. I would like to begin by quoting from the presidential address of a past president of the American Cancer Society, Dr Pentegrass, a man who has had a profound influence on my own thinking:

Now finally, I would like to leave you with a thought that is very near to my heart. Anyone who has had an extensive experience in the treatment of cancer is aware that there is a great difference among patients. I personally have observed cancer patients who have undergone successful treatment and were living and well for years. Then an emotional stress, such as the death of a son in World War II, the infidelity of a daughter-in-law or the burden of long employment seem to have been precipitating factors in the reactivation of their disease, which then resulted in death. There is solid evidence that the course of disease in general is affected by emotional stress. Thus, we as doctors may begin to emphasize treatment of the patient as a whole as well as the disease from which the patient is suffering.

We may learn how to influence general body systems and through them modify the neoplasm which resides within the body. As we go forward in this pursuit of the truth to try to stamp out cancer, searching for new means of controlling growth both within the cell and through the systemic influences, it is my sincere hope that we can widen the quest to include the distinct possibility that within one's mind is a power capable of exerting forces which can either enhance or inhibit the progress of this disease.

In the last few years, the literature relating directly and indirectly to the study of cancer has been deluged with papers and articles arguing that the personalities, emotions and distresses of patients are significant factors both in the development and the progress of cancer. This has proved equally so in the study of human beings as well as in experimentation on animals. Roughly, there have been over two hundred articles, and all of them conclude that emotional stress is a factor in the onset or the progress of the disease. So the question is not whether there is a relationship between emotional stress and cancer, but whether there is a direct causal link from the first to the second – and, if so, what that 'link' is.

The 'Cause' of Cancer

Based on my reading and experience with cancer patients, the most important single factor in precipitating the disease is the loss of a significant object. This may be a loved one, it may be a real or imaginary object, it may be a job, it may be a person. The loss precipitates a diagnosis of cancer between six and eighteen months thereafter. The result, however, is not necessarily overt symptoms of cancer; frequently cancer is asymptomatic at the time a patient is first seen by the doctor.

The 'cause' may not be the loss as such. Many of us lose objects and people we value. It is rather the individual's *response* to the loss. In other words, the sense of loss needs to be great enough to generate a feeling of helplessness and hopelessness. When we look more closely at this sense of loss, we often find a life pattern. There have been a number of controlled studies (using matched normals) which have demonstrated this point. In any event, nothing further need be added to make the point: cancer is stress-related and stress itself is often manifested in a pattern in the lives of some subjects. Our interest is how far psychological stress is implicated.

I believe that there is a 'cancer personality'. I made this assertion once on a television show. I was immediately quizzed and was amazed to learn that a former professor of mine had categorically denied its existence on the same show a few weeks earlier. My amazement stemmed from the fact that the literature abounds with descriptions of personality factors. Moreover, I had personally verified its existence in my own research. My convictions are further reinforced by my own experience – I had cancer at the age of seventeen and can see how closely my personality then resembled the classical description. Some of the features of the cancer personality are a tendency to resent (that is, a tendency not to forgive), a tendency towards self-pity, and a marked inability to form and maintain meaningful relationships. Finally, nearly every patient has a poor self-image. I wish I could say that I did not have these traits at seventeen, but I know I did and still do residually. It takes continuous effort on my own part to reduce their impact. The malignancy in my own case has not recurred, which helps me to feel that I am making some progress in ridding myself of these undesirable traits.

A final point: almost everyone has some of these traits in them – the important issue is the extent to which they are predominant characteristics.

If personality has an influence on this disease, how can personality be modified to forestall its occurrence? This is the heart of the matter. Undoubtedly, as I and some of my colleagues know too well, modifying personality is an extremely difficult task.

The Role of 'Belief-Systems'

The most embracing and cohesive term I can find to discuss my views is 'expectancy'. What I study is the patient's belief-system – the attitudes to life in general, and to cancer in particular, that patients possess. Belief-systems are dynamic, not static, processes; though they are more rigid in some than in others. Cancer patients typically see the disease as something which attacks them – some external agent. None the less, though they see it as essentially an invader, they feel that it is devouring them internally. And they often feel this is a process over which they have little or no control. Attitudes to treatment vary. Those around the cancer patient tell him (perhaps feel obliged to tell him) that he is going to be miserable. Those around him do not necessarily say such things directly, but they may remind him how it was with Aunt Mary. Consequently, through friends and acquaintances, any views the patient may previously have held about the existence and effectiveness of cancer therapies are rapidly eroded. As a result, when we attempt to change a patient's belief-system, we must also deal with the belief-systems of his friends and relatives. But what about the belief-system of the physician?

Many doctors would disagree, but the overwhelming evidence is that the belief-system of the physician plays an integral part in the patient's response to treatment. Again, it is not a question of whether the physician's attitude has an effect, but of how much effect it has.

What about my own belief-system as a physician? All human beings have cancer cells within them. The problem is not the cancer cells but the breakdown of the body's ability to deal with them and to rid itself of disease. I see cancer, therefore, as having much in common with diseases like tuberculosis, the common cold and so forth. We are continually exposed to many damaging agents both from within and from without, but it is only when we become susceptible to them that the disease actually develops.

What are my views on treatment? I believe that the best tool I can use is radiation treatment. It can destroy a malignancy and return a patient to a more healthy condition. But radiation therapy is not the only weapon; it should be augmented by the patient's belief in his own ability to get well. My belief that the patient has it within his power to get well is based on many factors – evidence from biofeedback, from the various meditative procedures and from experience with spontaneous remission. The patient possesses tremendous potential to influence his or her own vital forces to affect any malady, and that includes cancer. The evidence for this view is overwhelming. Naturally, my own beliefs are subject to dynamic and real influences. When several of my patients die, my wife seems to neglect me and then my business life is afflicted by set-backs. Those factors in turn influence my ability to effectively relate to my patients. If this is true, the responsibility on the physician is heavier than most would be willing to accept. But this does not affect the validity of the proposition.

The Treatment

The unconventional tool I use in the treatment of cancer, apart from irradiation, is 'relaxation and mental imagery'. Other people prefer terms such as meditation, hypnosis, self-hypnosis, autogenic training and so on.

In regular sessions with a patient I ask the patient to practise simple muscle relaxation, focusing on breathing. Then I have him mentally picture his cancer – picturing it the way it seems to him – and the way he views the treatment, how he sees the body and body-cells operating against the malignancy, and so on. I try to get him to produce mental descriptions of all aspects of the disease. Through these techniques, the patient begins to activate his motivation to be well and to arouse emotions and problems into consciousness.

A Case History

The case considered is that of a throat cancer patient. The

patient tells me that all his life he has felt stress in his neck – he has had frequent sore throats, including laryngitis. (This need not always be the case with throat patients, incidentally, but is often the case.) He has the feeling that whenever he gets into a difficult situation, his throat will tighten up. First, I try to teach him methods of relaxation. The hardest part of his anatomy for him to relax proves to be his throat. Soon he will be able to do this in quiet, controlled circumstances, during therapy for instance. But when it is time for him to leave and go home, his throat begins to tighten up. But now he is aware of this. He understands what happens to him and gradually, consciously, he can begin to do something about reducing the tightness whenever it occurs. Even if he fails to control it altogether, he is at least aware of the failure.

But then he notices that when he gets home and sees his wife, the tightness arises again. He consciously tries to relax it. Things are okay for a while again, until the wife brings up the subject of their daughter. Now his throat is really tense. Then his wife says their unmarried daughter's pregnancy test was positive. Now the patient cannot breathe or swallow or cough properly, and he goes into spasms. Now he has to work again to try to calm down, and perhaps can soon relax again. A sequence of events like this is typical. The area of the body that expressed the disease is usually the area which expresses tension.

Treatment Results

We have found that in changing the patient's belief-systems visual presentations are very effective. I show the patient a series of slides. The slides are in fact the best ones I have representing my most successful cases. They show 'before' and 'after' pictures of successfully treated cancer.

For instance, I show slides of a patient who had cancer of the roof of the mouth. After only one week of treatment, its action is significantly decreased compared with its initial appearance. After four weeks of treatment, the growth has disappeared and the area has healed over, though it is not yet fully normal. Ten weeks after treatment the cancer can scarcely be seen. I have similar slides for a number of widely differing cases. In one case a man had severe warts on both hands. The results achieved were striking. Yet another set of slides shows the course of a very large anal cancer in a woman fifty-five years of age. After four weeks of treatment, there was very marked improvement. By the time the treatment was completed, virtually all trace of the cancer had disappeared.

This is an excellent instance of what I want my patients to see – complete disappearance of a very severe malignancy with no complications. A striking series is focused on a twelve-year-old with a large scrotal cancer. He had had previous surgery, but the condition had recurred. Two weeks after we began treatment, the cancer had begun to reduce noticeably. Further improvement was recorded after a further week of treatment. At this time, however, he became difficult to manage; an ulcerated condition developed on top of the cancer – a serious complication. We had him back for basic supportive therapy and did what we could to reassure his parents. We had no idea at this time how the case was going to go. A month later we noted improvement again. Treatment continued. At the completion of treatment the outlook was favourable. A month thereafter, no cancer was discoverable by surgical examination.

There have been several studies correlating the attitudes of cancer patients with their response to treatment. I decided to see whether I could confirm the findings of those studies. First, we developed a five-point prognosis grading scale running from doubly positive to doubly negative. Each of five doctors gave his vote on each patient, based on his own clinical judgment and experience. From these we then calculated a single 'prognosis' for each patient. We also utilized a four-point scale ranging from 'poor' to 'excellent', on which we rated the patient's response to treatment. Once again, a single score was calculated from the combined projections. At the end of eighteen months we had evaluated 152 cases. Briefly, what a statistical analysis of the data shows is essentially a one to one correlation between the patient's attitude to treatment and his response to treatment. Patients with good attitudes had good responses, those with poor attitudes had poor responses.

The 'Cure' of Cancer

I am often asked about cancer 'cures'. It is a poor term; it means very little. The only way you can be sure you have 'cured' a patient is if he eventually dies without cancer cells present at autopsy. Because diagnosis is so tricky, cancer therapists prefer simply to speak of five years without remission, ten years without remission, and so on. A cure is a necessarily provisional condition.

An example will illustrate some of the difficulties. The best patient I ever had was a 35-year-old black model – by best I mean that she initially had the most serious disease and initially displayed the best response to treatment.

When she first came to me, she was already seriously ill, but it was not yet appropriate for me to treat her. I did, however, establish a good rapport with her and discussed her own ability to deal with the disease – to get 'in touch' with the treatment she was receiving. One day her husband came to pick her up from my office. They fought (almost physically) in the office and in front of a stranger. There probably was a great degree of stress in their household. When I saw her next, a few months later, I began to treat her. The disease had continued to progress. It had spread to her brain and to her bones. She was in severe pain, could neither speak nor eat and was confined to bed. Fortunately she could hear. She became extremely positive and optimistic about what was going to happen. After a few radiation treatments, she was sitting up, eating and moving around in a wheel-chair. At the end of the second week she was pain-free and was walking, almost dancing.

She then went home, pain-free and under no medication. This was the most dramatic response I have ever seen. She was dead within a month.

Carl's experience with his 'favourite' patient is not unusual with healers, of all types. As long as disease is correctly thought of as maladaptation, rather than an eradicable physical condition, disease will always be with us – and that is an unfortunate but irresolvable fact. A disease-free society will never be achieved. Disease is a function of maladaptation. The diseases of the 'hunting' cultures yielded to changes in lifestyle that were introduced with the industrial revolution. But, in turn, new diseases emerged as industrialization became more widespread. Today as we move into a post-industrial era, most of the diseases associated with industrialization have been controlled – and we now face new diseases which reflect our failure to adapt to post-industrial stresses. The key to health may be in a clearer understanding of the dialectic between the human species and its environment, physical and cultural.

The Interconnectedness of the Human Species and Nature

Many medicines in the past recognized the intimate interrelationship between man and Nature. Modern medicine, however, largely ignores these factors, choosing instead to try to cure the animal whose environment ravages him. Nevertheless, some of the ancient wisdom is being rediscovered.

The body is a mirror of patterns and cycles. There are certain rhythms and cycles which are rooted in our biology. Gay Gaer Luce, in *Body Time,* reviews the research which has been done – how mood, performance, activity and tactility all fluctuate with time:

> Time is yet the most intimate and pervasive aspect of our lives, yet the language of our self-expectations is static. We traverse the life cycle from birth to maturity, aging, and death. We observe the round of seasons, the ceaseless alternation of day and night. We are touched by inner cycles of sleepiness and hunger, yet our self-image is as fixed as a photograph. We expect consistent feeling and behavior in family and friends. We aspire to undeviating performance at work, and measure our state of health against some static norm. Our habitual language imposes the expectations of a steady state. All of this hinders us from feeling our rhythmic nature.[6]

There is a rich literature on this subject. The human organism exists in a pulsating web of interactions with other animate life, with terrestrial and solar waves and radiations, and with man-made machines and equipment. The human animal throbs at its own rates, and projects, as well as receives, impulses. Most interactions take place at subconscious levels. An excellent example is the human reaction to 'infra-sounds' – frequencies at less than ten to twenty cycles per second, below the threshold of human hearing. As with many other recent discoveries, the initial revelation arose by chance. A Professor Gavraud from Marseilles always felt ill at work. Gavraud, a dedicated worker, decided to find out why. He soon located the problem – there was a low frequency vibration in his office, issuing from an air conditioner on top of the building directly across the street. The rhythm – seven cycles per second – made him ill. Gavraud's nausea has been confirmed by other studies – low frequency sound waves do affect the body, and in some cases illness can result.[5] The case of Professor Gavraud is just one of the illustrations in Lyall Watson's book *Supernature,*[6] an extended discussion of the interconnectedness of the human species and its environment. In describing his thesis, Watson argues that:

> ... Too often we see only what we expect to see: our view of the world is restricted by the blinkers of our limited experience, but it need not be this way. Supernature is nature with all its flavors intact waiting to be tasted. I offer it as a logical extension of the present state of science as a solution to some of the problems with which traditional science cannot cope, and as an analgesic to modern man.
> I hope that it will prove to be more than that. Few aspects of human behavior are so persistent as our need to believe in things unseen – and as a biologist, I find it hard to accept that this is purely fortuitous. The belief, or the strange things to which this belief is so stubbornly attached, must have real survival value, and I think that we are rapidly approaching a situation in which this value will become apparent. As man uses up the resources of the world, he is going to have to rely more and more on his own. Many of these are at the

moment concealed in the occult – a word that simply means 'secret knowledge' and is a very good description of something that we have known all along but have been hiding from ourselves.[7]

In the essay which follows Lyall Watson amplifies these themes, with special attention to issues relating to health. But in doing so, he also provides a general critique of science.

IS PRIMITIVE MEDICINE REALLY PRIMITIVE?

Lyall Watson, Ph.D.

Some years ago, I was standing on a street corner in Madras watching a man earn his living in what seemed to me the most difficult way possible. He had meat skewers stuck through his cheek and out the other side. Safety pins were laced in and out of his tongue. Through the soft parts of his arms and legs he had placed knives. Yet these are common observations in most cities in the East. What was less common was that I was joined by a group of tourists. Included in this American party was a young girl who was so upset by what she saw that she sought defence in rudeness. She said things like, 'It's all done with mirrors. They're rubber spikes. Isn't he an ugly little man anyway?' Until that moment I had not been sure whether the fakir understood English. But he did.

First, he removed and put down his hardware. Then he walked over to the girl and asked if she were a Christian. She said she was. He asked her to define a Christian. In a few sentences he had led her to a point where she was telling him about the crucifixion. She concluded, showing the fakir her hands, 'And then they put nails through his hands.' I guessed what was going to happen. Her hands filled with pools of blood. She took one look and collapsed in a faint, the blood spilling down her dress. Her shaken party carried her away.

I stayed on to talk to the fakir about the incident. He regretted his action, saying that he should not have allowed himself to be provoked. I saw him several times in the next days and got to know him quite well. Eventually he took me to meet his family in a little village between Madras and Pondichery. All the family could perform these remarkable physiological feats. They took it as a matter of course. One morning I was sitting with his young son in the garden when the boy picked up an earthenware jug of water, poured some into his hand and drank it, not by lifting his hand to his mouth but by sucking the water in through the pores of his skin. It gurgled briefly on his hand and then was gone. I asked if he could do it again. He did, using the other hand. That day was a major turning point for me. Watching that ten-year-old, suddenly my years of university training seemed to have been a terrible waste of time. I would much rather be able to do what that boy did than know what I know. I am trained as a natural scientist. Yet science considers what that boy did as unnatural. It considers it worse than impossible; it considers it to be outside of science.

The attitude of the girl in my story is typical of many of my contemporaries. Something is impossible, therefore it cannot happen. This is, of course, a basic dilemma – one that I had to face at the time. In the West we have a dogmatic certainty about reality which we have acquired from our cultural and educational background. We have firm, preconceived ideas about what constitutes fact and what fiction. But there are no absolute realities. Our description of reality is only one of several possible descriptions, our truth only one truth. It therefore becomes necessary for each of us to reassess what he or she is prepared to believe, and on what grounds.

Look again at Western science. You will find that a great deal of it is, despite appearances, a matter of blind faith. We believe things because they have been demonstrated by the scientific method. Yet what is that method? It is based on observation – the observation of a particular kind of material reality. The theories which it sets out to prove or disprove are equally rooted in that same materialism. A proof is merely one aspect of that reality by reference to another aspect of the same reality.

Knowledge in the West is accreted by an elaborate system of, usually rival, research projects. Researchers live in the delicious hope of discrediting each other's work. Papers and theories are submitted to eminent referees for, hopefully, constructive comment and criticism. The whole process, we believe, ends with the selection of what is true and the rejection of what is false. However, I have deep doubts whether that is what actually occurs. The establishment of a truth often is a political process, not a scientific one – for it is based on the word, sometimes the whim, of personalities. One relies on somebody else. For example, I am prepared to take the word of the Professor of Physics at Cambridge, but I ignore the view of the Professor of Metaphysics at the University of Transcendental Meditation. The former claims that an electron is a wavicle, essentially only describable mathematically. The latter tells me that an electron is the soul of a departed person made manifest in light. Many experiments in physics and the other sciences turn out to be really experiments in professors.

My friends in Madras do not have these problems. I envy them enormously. They have no difficulty in coming to terms with a talent that can take in water through the palm of one's hand or push blood out of someone else's. They rely on intuition. Their intuition tells them that the universe is seamless and that movement between all parts of it is readily possible. Our intellect blocks us from this kind of appreciation. The intellect insists on a division between 'I' and everything else in the universe – and equally between all the different aspects of the universe. This restrictive and divisive approach to information is perhaps dictated by one sense in particular – by sight. Our wide array of senses is subordinated to this one sense, so much so that in most cases we trust only it. So we say 'Seeing is believing,' and 'I would not have believed it if I had not seen it.' When we ask for proof, we say 'Show me.' We ignore the possible truth of the view 'I would not have seen it if I had not believed it.'

We tend to perceive only what we can first conceive. So when Charles Darwin went to Tierra del Fuego in the *Beagle,* the Indians there could not see his ship. They had boats of their own, but they were small canoes. Their imaginations could not envisage a ship of the *Beagle's* size – not until, that is, they were taken out in the boats and allowed to touch it.

Too often, then, we see what we expect to see and only what we expect to see.

We run into further problems when we try to encode an experience in words, especially a total experience. For example, a child wakes at dawn, goes out tracking rabbits in the dew, smells the damp patches of fresh brown and white mushrooms, tastes the bloom on a grape, fresh and cool from the vine. He meets a couple of his friends, they hug, wrestle, and run down a hill together to swim in a stream still cool and milky from the mountain snows. Then they lie in the sun drying on a log, listening to a band somewhere in the distance. When the child gets home his mother asks where he has been. 'Out.' What did he do? 'Nothing.' Or, if pressed for a 'real' answer, the child might say 'Swimming.' That will satisfy the mother. The child knows how inadequately words express his experience. He does not try. The intellect, however, feels obliged to try for a description – and founders in the attempt. What is the point of this exercise?

An intuitive approach to knowledge never runs into this difficulty. All major advances in science are made intuitively. They are rarely made by the intellect travelling well-used paths. What is needed is the intuitive leap through the very frontiers of knowledge. Why is our whole education system designed to conceal this fact? Universities and schools are designed to advance the intellect at the expense of intuition. Limits are created artificially; when the only limits we are obliged to encounter are those of our own imagination. We entirely ignore the possibility that a child daydreaming in class may be using his brain more productively than a child who is paying attention.

This restriction of view is particularly evident in our notions of health and disease. Maybe this is why we make so little progress in true healing. I have begun to look at health from a more anthropological point of view. It soon becomes apparent that there is almost no such thing as absolute disease. What is considered to be illness varies from culture to culture. What one society calls neurosis, for example, another calls religious conviction. Culture also has a marked impact on the manifestation of the disease. There is evidence that attacks of coronary thrombosis are as common in African

tribes as here in the West, for example. Yet the expectations
are different. No one expects to *die* of a heart attack in
Africa, and so they rarely do. Cultural behaviours and
disease are equally closely linked. In our society, the incidence of angina is greatest among harassed businessmen.
Naturally, the most important of all the cultural effects on
disease lies in the theory of disease to which the culture
subscribes. Is it caused by witchcraft, God's anger,
bacteria – what? The answer to that question depends on the
kind of help that is available to treat disease. Our culture
believes that illness is caused by bacteria and germs. We
believe further that the patient, by those agencies, can
transmit his disease to others. We therefore isolate him in a
sterile environment – away from germs and also away from
people in general. We do this in the case of mental illness as
well, though for reasons of metaphorical rather than literal
infection. We separate the patient and society. Primitive
cultures rarely do this. Their response to sickness is to bring
the patient still further into society, to make him feel even
more that he belongs. Navajo Indians bring as many as a
thousand patients to a curing session, which is a wild and
wonderful party. Action of this kind reinforces social bonds.
In a wide variety of cultures illness is commonly divided into
three classes. There are natural ills like burns, fractures, food
poisonings and so on. These are fairly readily treated by a
tribe specialist, often a herbalist, in time-honoured ways. A
second type is normally described as a 'dull' illness or sickness. These are the ones that hang around for long periods
and are hard to cure. Most cultures feel these are caused by
some kind of imbalance. There is an attempt to redress the
balance, usually by group action of the kinds I have just
noted. The treatment is often strikingly effective. The third
type of illness is the sudden or 'sharp' incapacitation, seizure
or whatever. Usually these are held to be of external
origin – there has been a bewitchment in some sense. These
cases are handled by a medicine man who administers some
sort of social shock treatment.
There is a certain balance and logic in this view of illness and
its treatment, if not altogether rational in our terms. The
culture pinpoints the source of the disease, allows for its

expression, and provides a cure with a built-in reinforcement. I find it hard to regard this system as primitive. It seems to me to compare favourably with our care system, under which patients can leave hospital as ill, or more ill, than when they entered it.

I have recently made a study of one primitive system of healing, in the Philippine Islands. The cultural history of these people is something of a patchwork. An initially aboriginal-negrito people, some of whom still live in the mountains, has been overlaid or displaced by invasions, primarily from the Malay peninsula. Subsequently the Spanish arrived with their strongly Catholic culture. More recently there has been an American invasion.

There is a system of modern medicine, a flourishing medical association and so on. All Philippinos, at least in the urban areas, have access to contemporary drug therapy treatment. This therapy has replaced most herbalist practice. However, the 'sharp' and 'dull' types of illness I spoke of earlier are still often treated by native healers, and very effectively. Many native healers have become Church-affiliated, and have accordingly gained in respectability. Nevertheless, on the smaller islands, away from the conurbations, you still can find the old, iconoclastic healers.

I found one such healer on the island of Mindaro. This man lives in a hut in the mountains. He is not a member of the Church or spiritist groups, nor is he active in the healing movement. He is a wild, long-haired isolate – though well-known in the area as a healer. People frequently approach him for healing but soon leave; he is what is called an 'absent' healer – he heals at a distance.

I personally experienced his power. I told him that I had a friend in Africa whom I would like him to help. He asked me in which direction Africa was and I pointed. He looked, nodded assent and asked for a sheet of paper. I gave him a sheet from my notebook which he rolled up into a simple sort of paper trumpet. Then he peered through this. 'She does not look very well, does she?' he said. 'Don't worry though. I can handle it. She has a stomach problem.' I agreed that she had a stomach problem, an infection. The healer then put the paper trumpet against his mouth and began to suck huge intakes of breath three or four times. Then his mouth appeared suddenly to fill with something; he spat it into a bowl. It was the most evil-smelling jollop I have ever come across. I thought he must have regurgitated this and immediately examined it. However, it did not have a stomach smell. It seemed to be a mixture of blood and pus. He emptied another pint of this muck from the trumpet and crumpled up the paper. We had about two pints of the stuff in the bowl. 'Fine, it's all over now,' said the healer. 'She is okay.'

A week later I reached town again. I immediately sent a cable to the girl. When I reached London, there was a letter from her. She said that she did not know what had happened but that she was feeling marvellous. Now, what can I say about this? I do not believe that the healer sucked pus eight thousand miles across the ocean. I do believe though that the healer – in common with many healers in the Philippines – materialized a substance. The explanation of the powers which the healer gave was inconsistent, however. He argued that he was just a channel; something worked through him. In this case he said it was the spirit of the wild tamaro – the buffalo I had come to the island to see. Before he found the paper trumpets, he had used a buffalo horn.

The healing movements in the Philippines actually began in France in the last century. A spiritualist, Alain Cardeque, believed that health was bestowed by the action and help of spirits who lived in an invisible world. The movement flourished briefly in France, then died out. But it survived in two main areas abroad – Brazil and the Philippines. Both territories, of course, have vigorous Catholic communities. They gave the spiritist movement the survival impetus it needed when it reached their shores. In both areas an indigenous healing movement also existed, on which to graft the new spiritism.

In the Philippines all the healers I worked with live on the northernmost island, Luson. The total population of the Philippines, on seven thousand islands, is forty million. Population is very unevenly distributed. Between Manila and Buggio are the lowlands of Pangansinan. All the healers I met seem to have originated, either by birth or training, from this small area. Few have had any formal education, and none of them know much about modern medicine. They live in simple houses in agricultural communities. They earn very little, asking for no payment, but accepting any donation the patient cares to make.

The healers have several things in common. They all use prayer as part of their ritual. The prayers may last a minute or so, or go on for hours. They all work in crowded, communal situations. As many as forty patients may be waiting their turn; and all see what goes on before their own treatment. A powerful process of reinforcement is at work; a high rate of exchange of information and experience. After a day in one of these rooms the observer feels that he has somehow contributed and feels absolutely drained, physically and emotionally.

The healers all cure in a kind of semi-trance. It is more of a dissociation than a full trance. All use the traditional 'laying on of hands', but each has his own individual ways and methods of stage management or window dressing. Josephine Sissons specializes in 'unwitching' – that is, the removal of foreign objects from patients' bodies. Usually she begins by stuffing cotton wool into a person's head or body. She might push it into one ear and withdraw it from the other. As she manipulates the wool going in, it actually disappears. I have watched this several hundred times from a distance of five or six inches. The cotton just dematerializes. The same piece of cotton wool does not come out the other side. I have used marked samples. The healer was surprised to learn this.

With the patient's mind prepared by her demonstration, and depending on her own diagnosis, Josephine will usually go on to 'remove' something from the patient's body. It might be a bundle of dried leaves. Or it might be a huge intact leaf ten to twelve inches long and without creases, so that it could hardly have been conventionally palmed. It might be an entire corncob, ten inches long complete with fruit, a plastic bag, a six-inch rusty nail, or a piece of glass. It could be almost anything you care to name. I do not think these objects are necessarily extracted from the sufferer's body. I believe they materialize at the interface between healer and patient. They are there from one moment to the next, between one frame of the film and the next. The method is very effective, perhaps because some tangible object is apparently removed.

Another healer, Juan Blanche, specializes in removing little things from the eyes. From the eye of an individual with conjunctivitis he might remove a bean-shaped, green, doughy mess. This seems to bring immediate remission of the problem. Again, I have watched Juan very closely – the materials do seem to just appear from under the eyelid. The healer points his finger, touches the eyelid, and out pops the substance.

Juan Blanche also has another remarkable skill. He can point or strike at the patient's body with his finger, a good foot or so from the actual body surface, and an incision appears. He can also use the finger of a bystander. The cut which appears is not deep and bleeds very little. It will not always be parallel with the movement made by the finger. But Juan does not touch the body. I underwent the process myself. A plastic sheet was laid across my chest, the healer moved his finger in my direction, and a cut appeared in my skin under the plastic. However, there was no mark of any kind on the plastic. You feel the cut appear, and although it is not particularly painful it takes a few days to heal.

Jose Mercardo gives spirit injections. He lines up patients in his clinic and walks along the row saying, 'Zip, zip, zip,' from distances of five to six feet. As he does this, he points his finger and each one feels a prick in the body at the point at which the finger is directed. Again, I wrapped my arm in plastic under my shirt and asked if I could be subjected. He performed the injection as described. I felt a prick in my arm and a spot of blood appeared beneath the plastic and my shirt. No mark was on the shirt, but this time the plastic was drilled as though by a needle, clean through several layers. This occurred at a distance of six feet.

Yet another kind of treatment involves actual manipulations on or of the body surface. This kind of treatment is the most common, the most dramatic and, for perhaps obvious reasons, the most effective. The healer begins to knead and manipulate the patient's body surface – often the abdomen, perhaps because this is soft and easy to work with. He may begin by having a piece of cotton wool in his hands, soaked in water or oil. Or he may have nothing at all in his hands. The healer will knead the surface as though preparing dough for bread. As he does this, blood, or a red liquid, suddenly appears. He may declare the operation complete at this point. If he continues, however, some kind of tissue soon materializes. Often it looks as if the body has been opened at this point, but I am fairly sure that in most cases this does not occur. The tissue either is, or closely resembles, a mesentery – the membrane that attaches organs to the body wall. However, I believe that this material is expressed on the body, not in the body. The tissue, on analysis (healers usually do not object to one taking the substance away), may prove to be human, or it may turn out to be goat, pig or chicken – or, in one case, sheep. (There are no sheep on the islands, incidentally.) The fact that the tissue is not human does not necessarily mean that the healer has been cheating. This assumption has frequently been made in the past. I believe it to be unfounded. I have watched hundreds of these operations, as I said, and I can personally swear that there is no sleight of hand. It is not, as far as I was able to observe – and I did observe very, very closely – either produced or produceable from the clothes of the healer or from beneath the table. It simply seems to appear on the surface of the patient's body.

Under the mesentery or tissue, however, something further may occur. Sometimes a lump will arise. It just seems to grow up from within the body of the patient. Then the healer may cut the tissue, the actual living flesh of the patient this time, and lift out the internal tissue or substance with a pair of forceps. These objects are tumours. I have kept and examined several. They really are tumours. Again they need not be human, but they are tumours. One patient had been previously diagnosed as suffering from a fibroid tumour of the uterus. When she was X-rayed after the healing operation, that particular complication appeared to have totally vanished. In her case, then, some actual penetration of the body would seem to have occurred.

In these and other operations, substantial pieces of tissue are somehow produced. Any blood that is produced seems to clot more quickly than one would expect in normal surgery. Actual penetration of the body may sometimes occur. It is unwise in my opinion, however, to focus on the question of penetration. I believe our interest should focus on the problem of materialization. I am not qualified to say how much, or what kind of, healing took place as a result of these various operations – though I understand that there is notable remission in some sixty per cent of cases. I do feel qualified, however, to stress the matter of materialization. I do not believe that it is conjuring; I believe it is real magic. One can also see operations on cysts. Again the incision is made without touching. After that, natural methods are employed. The cyst is squeezed and evacuated. No attempt is made at sterilization, although a Bible is frequently held over the wound. Dirt and germs are everywhere. Yet no infection follows. Additionally, though the healer does some pretty rough and radical manipulation and exploration of the wound, no pain is sensed by the patient. Sometimes after an operation a wound will be cauterized in a simple way. A piece of cotton wool may be burned and dabbed on the wound and a bandage applied over the top.

Among the many questions which arise are how do these patients and healers control pain and why can't everyone do it? We require anaesthetics – but then, what is an anaesthetic? The drugs which produce anaesthesia are a wide range of substances with little in common. Perhaps they work partly because we believe in them. Maybe anaesthesia is really an altered state of mind. Drugs may somehow help to create that state of mind. We know of course that it can be created as well by hypnosis and acupuncture.

Why is there no infection after these operations? This is harder to understand. We know, or believe we know, that staphylococcus produces boils. Apparently such germs are always present on our skin. What gives them their chance? Philippine healers agree that imbalance gives them their chance – and they would treat boils by attempting to locate and correct the imbalance.

Now we come to Tony Agpao. He is the most important and most advanced healer in the Philippines. The other fifteen or so healers I worked with all seemed to perform in a slightly dissociated or trance-like state. They do not appear to have much conscious control over the often complex acts they perform. But Tony Agpao is different. He seems to be fully conscious and in control. In my work with him I was able to exercise a high degree of experimental supervision, which was not possible in other cases. He would come to a hotel room of my choosing and work on a bed of my choosing. He would turn up in a short-sleeved shirt and a pair of trousers and agree to be stripped and searched before beginning. I bought and provided the cotton wool that he used. I also provided the water myself, and so on.

I have a film of him at work under these conditions. In the film he wears a short-sleeved shirt. He waves his arms in the air before beginning and then performs an operation on a German woman suffering from a liver complaint. A German surgeon, a specialist, was present during the operation and we have his comments.

The surgeon tells us that the patient, forty-seven years old, had suffered for twenty-nine years from colongitis – a disease of the duct of the liver. In 1952, her gall-bladder was removed because of inflammation and daily attacks of colic. In spite of this operation, substantial problems remained. She had pronounced sensitivity to pressure on the liver. She could not take fats, cabbage, coffee and many other foods, and still suffered from occasional attacks of colic accompanied by pains in the right shoulder blade. In 1953, she was involved in a serious motor accident which produced a severe disability of the spine. Since then, continual pain in her spine has forced her to give up her occupation.

These are the further comments of the surgeon who watched the operation on the woman's liver by Tony Agpao:

> What we saw here, the intervention of a healer of this sort, cannot be explained nor understood by conventional or academic medicine. The word 'intervention' is used and not 'operation' because there are fundamental differences between the two procedures. We saw first a piece of tissue that had apparently been pulled out. I judged it to be a portion of intestine with mesentery. Black spots were present, being blood clots resulting

from pulling or tearing. In conventional, academic medicine pieces of tissue from the liver are virtually always taken only for diagnostic purposes. The purpose of this present intervention is therefore without meaning for the conventional physician. That is not at all to say that this type of treatment is without therapeutic value. In fact the patient was healed of all her problems or complaints, except for a minor complaint about her spine. Since her treatment the patient can eat all foods, including fats and other indigestible items, and can again tolerate coffee and alcohol. What was noteworthy in the treatment or intervention was when the hand was removed from the body, no edge of the wound was visible. It is impossible to discern where the blood came from. Why the various manipulations are necessary I cannot explain. The healer pulled out a second piece of tissue, which I believe was part of the mesentery. After parting this tissue, an assistant removed part of what seemed to be the liver with forceps. According to conventional medicine this procedure is unthinkable, since any gross injury to the liver leads to profuse bleeding which can hardly be stopped.

The patient herself described what happened as follows:

I did not feel the opening of the abdomen, but I did feel it when the body was opened. I could feel him go under my ribs with his hands to do something. It was not painful. It was not even painful when he took something out. Did you notice in the film that he cut something off with scissors? I noticed afterwards that something had been taken out. Somehow I felt it must be a large piece that was taken from deep in the body. In fact I said, 'Now he is taking something out,' and immediately those who were watching said, 'Now it is coming out.'

The patient was asked if she thought it possible that the entire experience she had had could have been somehow produced while the skin remained intact and was merely manipulated:

No. That would have been virtually impossible. One can certainly feel whether a person is pressing on the body from the outside or whether he is inside the body. In this operation I could feel that what was taken out came from very deep in the body. Following this operation I had severe pain. After the piece was taken out of the body the witnesses, as well as I, heard him count one, two, three and he closed the wound so fast that I experienced very sharp pains.

The piece of removed tissue was diagnosed by a recognized medical laboratory. Their report reads: 'The fatty liver shows signs of chronic inflammation. There are also small nodules which suggest an earlier case of typhoid.'

Now, instead of attempting to dispel anyone's doubts, I shall stretch credulity still further. I want you to know that we experienced many strange occurrences during the whole filming and recording process. For example, the German camera team wanted to prove once and for all that a body really had been opened. They brought in a patient with an artificial metal hip. They felt that if this metal could be seen in the course of the filmed operation, it would be irrefutable evidence that the body had been opened. Finally, we obtained a healer who would open the body. This is one of the few cases where I am sure the body was opened – because I saw the metal and the outline of the prosthesis. At the critical moment when the camera zoomed in to record this, the lights failed. Three days of filming without one mishap – and now, precisely at this moment, a breakdown.*

Here is another example. The patient of an Italian surgeon had a gall-stone. During a psychic operation Tony Agpao produced from this patient a gall-stone of rather unusual shape. The surgeon took it. He said that he had pre-existing

* This failure of equipment, incidentally, both in general and at crucial moments during research, is reported by many research workers in the psychic field. It appears to happen far more often than chance would warrant. 'Sceptics will, perhaps not unfairly, be inclined to sneer; but the likelihood of a world-wide conspiracy by scientists and technicians of otherwise high repute is frankly rather small. Probably what we see here are the side effects of the focusing of unusual and currently little-understood forces.

X-rays of this stone and that he was now in a position to compare the pictures with the actual stone. He placed the stone in a specimen jar which he put in his pocket. He flew back to Rome. When he got there, the still sealed specimen jar was empty. There it is. I understand that when material evidence or experience proves as insubstantial as this, proves unavailable for instrumentation and testing, that it is easy to dismiss the whole enterprise as fraudulent. I am satisfied from my own experience, however, that this is not the case. What we seem to have in the Philippines is of obvious importance. It is perhaps the first non-narcotic method of what Castaneda called 'stopping the world.' As a former – or perhaps still current – scientist, I understand that doubt has always been the most valuable and powerful weapon in the scientist's arsenal. Only by exercising rigorous doubt or testing can one arrive at the final truth. My view now is that this rampant doubt has been concealing large areas of information and knowledge from us. It is becoming increasingly obvious to me that a positive mental or emotional bias can be helpful in exploring some of these areas we have looked at tonight. Perhaps faith must become an essential item of our protocol.

What I am asking for is a return to alchemy. I believe the alchemists had the balance between scientific and spiritual exploration just about right. It is the notion and practice of balance which is so badly lacking in our disciplines. I believe that medicine and science are meaningless without 'magic'.

As Lyall Watson says, some phenomena 'stretch the credulity'. But the point is that 'interconnectedness' yields many phenomena – not all of which so 'stretch the credulity'. There are many pedestrian factors which deserve more attention. Light is one of them. John Ott, Director of the Environmental Health and Light Research Institute in Sarasota, Florida, was originally scheduled to participate in the May Lectures. Due to unforeseen circumstances he was unable to do so. But if he had, he would have discussed his research on the effect of light on health. His principal theme,

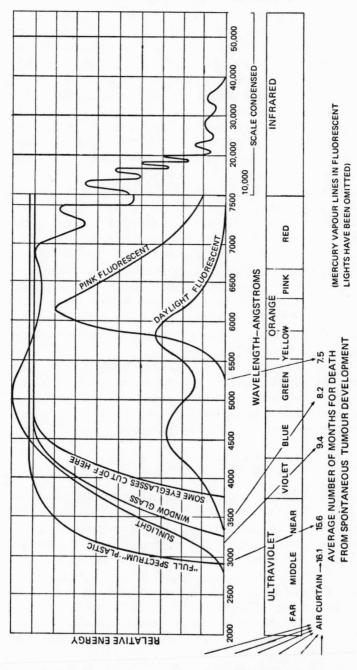

FIG. 2 INFLUENCE OF WAVELENGTHS OF LIGHT ON SPONTANEOUS TUMOUR DEVELOPMENT IN C₃H MICE

as articulated in his book *Health and Light*,[8] is that natural light is healthier than artificial light. In one of his more thorough studies, Ott investigated the influence of wave lengths of light on spontaneous tumour development in C_3H mice. The chart opposite (Figure 2), which is relatively clear, is reproduced from *Health and Light*.

Ott has also examined the human response. For example, he reports anecdotally on a potential relationship between the use of full-spectrum lighting and the contraction of flu in one business:

> During the winter of 1968-1969 a serious outbreak of Hong Kong flu swept the country. Florida was no exception. The Health Department reported 5 percent of Sarasota County – or 6,000 people – sick with the flu at one time. Employee illness caused the temporary closing of one supermarket, a social club, and the shutdown of two areas of the Sarasota Memorial Hospital because sixty-one nurses were out with the flu.
>
> Obrig Laboratories, located just north of Sarasota, is one of the largest manufacturers of contact lenses and has approximately one hundred employees. During the entire flu epidemic not one employee was absent because of any flu type ailment, according to Philip Salvatori, Chairman of the Board.
>
> Obrig Laboratories was the first to design a new building using full-spectrum lighting and ultraviolet-transmitting plastic panes throughout the entire office and factory areas. The added ultraviolet seemed to tie in closely with the results noted at the 'Well of the Sea' restaurant in Chicago. Mr. Salvatori also mentioned that the Obrig employees had not been given any mass inoculation against the Hong Kong flu, although some individuals may have received shots from their private physicians. Mr. Salvatori also commented that everyone seemed happier and in better spirits under the new lighting, and that work production had increased by at least 25 percent.[9]

Ott's work establishes a link between the nature and quality of light and health status. But more rigorous research has to be done – at a minimum, however, his research should elicit more.

'Energy' was a word and a concept frequently used during the May Lectures programme. Yet it was seldom used in the same way by the various participants. There was a tacit assumption that many of the phenomena under examination – 'psychic' healing, plant and human 'communication', field effects and so on – were somehow derivations of a larger, more embracing concept – perhaps an undefinable form of energy. It was also agreed that the species was subject to electromagnetic field effects which could not be fully explained given the state of the art. But whatever terms are used, the concept of 'energy' was a cornerstone for much of the discussion and for some of the presentations. For example, E. Stanton Maxey, M.D., Fellow of the American College of Surgeons and a Diplomate of the American Board of Surgeons, summarized his presentation this way: 'Thought is a form of energy; it has universal "field" properties which both affect and are affected by intertwining gravity, sound, light, magnetic, electrostatic, life and other thought fields.' This is like Sir James Jeans's quote in the introductory essay (page 23).

Dr Maxey's presentation focused on the 'field' effects which bear upon human functioning. His presentation ranged far and wide, embracing some relatively conventional concepts such as magnetic fields, but also touching on less conventional subjects such as reincarnation. In short, his presentation was a pot-pourri with something for everybody. There was a constant, however: the 'interconnectedness of man and his environment'.

MAN, MIND, MATTER AND FIELDS
E. Stanton Maxey, M.D.

Thought is a form of energy; it has universal 'field' properties which, like gravitational and magnetic fields are amenable to scientific research. Thought fields survive death and are analogous to soul and spirit.

S. R. Dean[10]

Profound words such as these promise to shake, modify and enlarge the basic root assumptions with which man views himself. Physicians who practise psychiatry can ill afford ignorance of those scientific facts which elucidate soul qualities. Patients profit or suffer in direct relationship to their physician's expertise in matters of the mind as well as in all other branches of the medical arts.

What then is man? Biological man originates as a unicelled organism within the mother's womb. Darwinian theories teach a similar phylogenetic beginning. As an adult he is an extraordinarily complex organism consisting of billions of highly specialized cells, affixed to an internal skeleton permitting great mobility within his geographic environment. His sense organs permit him unparalleled environmental contact by way of touch, taste, hearing, sight and smell – all of which are poorly understood. Consciousness might be called man's sixth sense; by this it is meant that man is aware not only of his biological structure and, to some degree, his external environment, but he is also aware of the fact that he is aware. Scientists know of no other creature who is aware of his own awareness. The seventh sense which is postulated relates to man's awareness of his own soul – psyche, if you like. The sciences of psychology, psychiatry, parapsychology, psychometry, psychotronics, psychokinesis, metapsychiatry and a host of others have come into being to explain to man his awareness of his own soul.

A proper sense of perspective may be achieved by admitting that the foregoing statements have both said a great deal and at the same time nothing at all. Let us illustrate. The human biological structure is by weight approximately eighty per cent water in one form or another; yet we know very little about water. Nobel Laureate Dr Linus Pauling proposed a clathrate hydrate structure which explains some physical properties of water, but not all. When water is broken up into small particles, the naturally occurring ionic charges may be either positive or negative. Some water freezes only at 169 degrees Fahrenheit below zero. Though chemically not changed, water after exposure to a thousand-oersted magnetic field dissolves scale from industrial boilers; and if fed to guinea pigs it causes them to diurese and become ill.

The progeny of these pigs will be undersized through the third generation. This exceedingly complex problem of water merely demonstrates the magnitude of the intricacy of the cellular systems and especially the multicellular organism called man.

Books have been written on the magnetic observations of various researchers on the cells of plants, animals and bacteria. Here, let us consider a human cell – say a leukocyte. This cell will have a negative charge at the nucleus with respect to the cellular protoplasm and cell membrane. It is as if the cell mimics in a microscopic way the charges on the surface of the earth as compared to the earth's ionosphere. Cellular metabolism and oxygen consumption seem to have a primary purpose – the function being that of pumping sodium, thus maintaining a high potassium concentration on one side of the cell membrane and a high sodium concentration on the other, with an associated marked ionic charge differential. Indeed, as long ago as 1943 Dr George Crile, founder of the Cleveland Clinic, stated that '... each living cell (is) a tiny electric battery generating its own current by chemical action.' This is precisely correct. Yet this concept, both confirmed and expanded by contemporary NASA researchers, was laughed at in his time. Dr Max Gerson, called by Dr Albert Schweitzer 'a medical genius who walked among us,' observed aberrations of sodium (Na+) versus potassium (K+) in cancer versus normal cells, and both evolved a demonstrably effective dietary cancer therapy and remarked on the essential life-sustaining qualities of the photon. With the advent of the electron spin laboratory came the brilliant and illuminating work of Professor Szent-Györgyi, who revealed the biological work functions of the cellular electron transfer.

Thus we have in man an astoundingly complex electrical being. Some of the isolated electrical qualities of man as a whole can be demonstrated in acupuncture point determinations. A field meter can be used to demonstrate man's total electrical field qualities. Indeed, Dr H. S. Burr was measuring various skin potentials in the mid-nineteen-thirties, and at that time correlated abnormal potentials with cancer of the female reproductive tract with a reported accuracy of ninety per cent. In physiological sleep man's skin resistance may go up by an order of magnitude and the electrical charge of the head versus the foot level may completely reverse itself. During dreaming there is a recordable theta or delta E.E.G. rhythm and an associated penile erection. Man is indeed astonishing from the electrical point of view, but when one associates cognitive processes with electrical functioning the puzzle deepens. Dr Andrija Puharich demonstrated that people could be taught to hear with electrical devices attached to the skin in areas unrelated to the acoustic nerve, and thus we see that the hearing mechanism comes into question in much the same way that perception of colours with one's fingers challenges orthodox optical neurological precepts. All men are, by experience, aware of their five senses – but where cognition of these senses takes place must, for the present, be left open for further study.

The Mind and Its Potential

Has a scientific measurement of cognition ever been accomplished? One must answer 'No,' yet each of us is aware of the 'I' within himself. The question must be formulated: 'Is awareness less a fact than that of which we are aware?' Is awareness a field phenomenon? Is the mind of man, the aware cognitive portion of his being, a function of the brain matter, or is it a field phenomenon associated at times with the brain but occasionally transcending, in a cognitive way, all usual geographic and time barriers? Examples of this transcendental mode may be found in the Bridie Murphy phenomenon, Dr Ian Stevenson's collection of some thirteen hundred cases 'suggestive of reincarnation', and Dr Dennis Kelsey's practical use of pre-incarnational psychic stresses as causes of his patients' contemporary emotional or mental disorders. Few psychiatrists seem aware of Dr Kelsey's work and his successful treatment track record. One is reminded of Dr Duncan Eve's admonition: 'There is no wrong way of treating fractures so long as success is achieved.' Does not the same logic apply when psychiatrists administer to the human psyche?

Those readers doubtful of the mind's ability to transcend

time may examine dreams in their content aspect. I have analysed many thousands of my own dreams and those of others. Here is one example which I recorded while I was an overnight guest of Dr Dennis Kelsey in Manhattan, on the night of May 26th, 1972.

> I dreamed of talking to a medium-built man who was telling me that he had a whole barn full of jet aircraft and a couple of Beechcraft (a small private aircraft). After we had talked I seemed to be floating in a garage over a light coloured sports car which had whitish chips of paint coming off all over. The top and the back window were apparent as I seemed to be over the top of the sports car in a paint shop.

The following day while checking out of La Guardia Airport, preparing my own aircraft for flight from New York to Hot Springs, Arkansas, I received a long distance telephone call from one Harold Isen of Washington, D.C. He had been informed by a mutual acquaintance, one Mr Carl Schleicher, that I would be going into Hot Springs and asked if I could stop in Washington, at Dulles International Airport, and pick him up. This I agreed to do. I was delayed in receiving clearance from New York by about thirty minutes. When I arrived at Dulles Airport, I found their Expo display was in progress and this caused considerable delay on departure. As I left the operational ramp, two men asked me if I was going west. I indicated that I was, and agreed to let them accompany me as they were both high-time jet pilots.
En route I asked these men to fly my aircraft, and then I sat in the back and began talking to them. When I inquired about their business, one George Eremea replied that he had a group of Falcons (a type of jet aircraft) in an operation at Little Rock. When I further inquired how he and his comrade, Glenn Germstead, would return from Hot Springs to Little Rock, he replied that he had already arranged for one of the Barons (a type of Beechcraft) to pick them up. At this point a recollection of my dream flooded into my mind and I, with considerable self-assurance, asked which of them drove sports cars. George Eremea, astonished, answered that he drove three of them. I then stated emphatically that one

of his cars needed painting. To this he replied, 'That is wrong.' After a short pause he then looked at me, completely amazed, and said, 'My wife has a cream-coloured Corvette which does indeed need painting as the paint is chipping off of it.'

Though statisticians may wish to figure the odds on the coincidences between this dream and the subsequent real experience, I – like the biblical King Saul – simply accept the precognitive aspect of the mind's dreaming capability. This assumption's validity is supported by observations of sophisticated contemporary researchers – including Dr E. Douglas Dean, Dr Stanley Krippner and Dr Hans Bender. All humans dream. Any of you may, by recording your dream scenarios, gain first-hand experience with the precognitive quality of your own mind's dreaming function. Readers doubting the dreaming mind's productivity may ponder the fact that physicist Niels Bohr received the Nobel Prize after revealing to the world his dream which depicted the structure of the atom.

Consider also 'out-of-body' experiences, in which certain people can voluntarily will their consciousness to travel through walls, over broad distances or into foreign lands, and while there accurately perceive events occurring in real time? More rarely, as with acute trauma or illness, individuals not normally having this free travelling mental faculty may similarly transcend the usual physical limitations of the mind's function. One neurosurgeon of my acquaintance was nonplussed when a head injury patient hallucinated in lucid archaic Spanish, a language to which the patient had never previously been exposed. Obviously, either the hundreds of such reports over many years result from some curious mass hysteria, or the mind can function apart from its usual connection with the cerebral cortex under some circumstances. Bob Monroe, an 'out-of-body' traveller himself, has, with expert assistance from contemporary physicists, assembled a complex electronic laboratory aimed at training people to achieve this mode of mind function.

Some of you will have investigated the mystifying capacities of clairvoyants, mediums and psychics. These people 'see' diseases and illness, perceive events at great distances, name names of persons unknown to them and accurately depict events of the past and of the future. At times, like the biblical Witch of Endor, they evidentially communicate with minds of people long dead and buried.

Both Friedrich Jurgenson and Konstantin Raudive have constructed devices through which 'voices' from the discarnate are recorded electronically without the intercession of a clairvoyant or medium.

With this scientific and quasi-scientific collation of reports of mind function in terms of reincarnation, dreams, out-of-body experiences and the recordings of non-physical minds via clairvoyants, many of you will by now be discomforted. Your 'root assumptions' as to the nature of man's existence will have been challenged. When sufficiently stimulated, you may investigate for yourselves both those aspects of this report which ring true, perhaps demonstrating some falsity, and those which ring false; in the latter case, verity will illuminate with a disconcerting frequency.

Some Thoughts About 'Field' Theory

Now let us examine man's conventional scientific root assumptions in areas of matter and fields. Man's waking environment includes fields of force involving gravity, magnetics, electrostatics, sound and light. His matter environment consists of atoms existing as solids, liquids and gases.

The terrestrial gravitational field varies with moon phasing, proximity to the sun and, to a lesser degree, planetary configurations. These variations affect the ticking of your watch, hence your sense of time. Even atomic function, such as in atomic clocks, varies with fluctuations in gravity fields. Albert Einstein postulated, and British astronomer Sir Arthur Eddington later showed, that light is bent in dense gravity fields. Astronomically, black holes in the heavens are thought to be regions so dense in gravity that light cannot escape from them. Gravity ties our bodies to the earth's surface ordinarily, but in space capsules it is absent. Its absence is, perhaps erroneously, thought to be associated with a myriad of physiological bodily changes.

What about sound? The normal human being perceives

sound at frequencies from about twenty to twenty-five thousand cycles per second. Plants are notably sound-sensitive, and with some exposures to Bach have grown up to thirty-five per cent faster; plants even incline towards speakers, clearly demonstrating their love of good music. Hard rock music, on the other hand, caused some plants to shrivel up and die. Non-living molecular sensitivity to sound is found in piezo-electric crystals whose electrons vibrate in response to sound; applications of this phenomenon provide us with microphones and ultra sound physiotherapy devices. Low frequency sound of three to five cycles per second (the brain's theta frequency) can rapidly kill human beings.

Now let us have a look at the earth's magnetics. The magnetic field varies in strength from about 0.3 to 1.5 gauss and emanates, except at the poles and the equator, at about sixty degrees from the earth's surface. This field has a normal resonance. No known living organism is immune to the magnetic field's effect. Fluctuating magnetic fields affect both electrons and ions, causing them to move at right angles to the lines of force of the field. Were this not so there would be no electric motors or generators. The effects of fluctuating

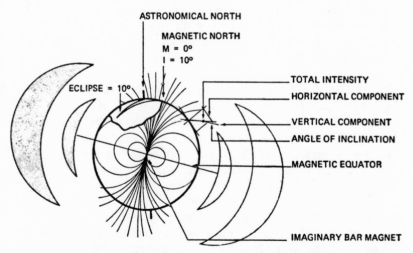

FIG. 3   SCHEMATIC DIAGRAM ILLUSTRATING MAGNETIC FIELD PRODUCED BY AN IMAGINARY BAR MAGNET AT THE EARTH'S CENTRE PLUS VAN ALLEN ZONES, INNER PROTONS AND OUTER ELECTRONS.

magnetic fields have biological and psychical interactions. Physicians generally are aware of the pH (hydrogen ion concentration) of the blood stream as a function of the normalcy of the bodily acid base mechanism. Few stop to consider the ion for what it is – 'an electrified particle formed when a neutral atom or group of atoms loses or gains one or more electrons.'

The fact that magnetic fields do indeed affect ions may be demonstrated by layering concentrated sulphuric acid carefully under diluted sulphuric acid and sprinkling in some inert powder as an observation tool; then an application of a magnetic field will result in rotation of one layer upon the other as the strength of the field increases. Reversal of the magnetic field will reverse the rotational direction. Similarly, red blood cells have been reported to rotate on their flat axis in vivo; in vitro they rotate if a magnetic field is applied. The direction of red blood cell rotation in vitro reverses if the field is reversed; an observation precisely to be expected of a body presenting ionic surface charges. Low frequency fluctuations of the terrestrial magnetic field in the three to five cycle per second range (this is the theta frequency of the E.E.G.) results in a prolongation of human reaction time by up to forty per cent, as determined by hundreds of thousands of observations. High frequency fluctuations have more destructive effects upon genetic chains than intense X-radiation, and such radio energy both causes cataracts and kills monkeys.

What about electrostatics? The earth may be viewed as a spherical capacitator. It is charged negatively at the surface; hence the symbol on ground leads of all electrical equipment is negative. At the ionosphere it is charged positively. The charge is immense. With proper, high-impedance volt meters the charge can be measured, and the gradient varies from approximately 100 to 25,000 volts per meter. That's right, up to 25,000 volts per meter. If you stand outside on a foggy day, the difference in potential may be from 100 to 35,000 volts at levels between the top of your head and the soles of your feet. Shocking? No. The conductivity of the air at close to sea level atmospheric pressures is so low that currents flowing through your body normally are not felt subjectively.

Magnetic fields and electrostatic fields, from the biological point of view, must be considered together as electromagnetic energy. This results from the effect that fluctuations of either electrostatic fields or magnetic fields have upon electrons and/or ions. Should a negative ion be subjected to a fluctuating magnetic field, that ion will oscillate on an axis which is at right angles to the magnetic field's lines of force. Since the electron has a negative charge this gyration per force generates a fluctuating electrostatic field which then is sensed along an axis at right angles to the fluctuating magnetic field. Such fluctuating fields together form a type of energy which we have long experienced as radio. Our terrestrial environment includes a considerable quantity of radio energy which constitutes one portion of our planet's environment. This natural radio energy is both created and perturbed by the function of our sun and the function and positions of some of our planets. Jupiter, for instance, generates 10^{14} times the radio energy present in the earth's Van Allen belts. Additionally, today we have the problem of radio pollution of our terrestrial environment with man-made radio energy. Dr Milton Zarat observed that monkeys subjected to the same type of radio energy as that to which sailors on aircraft carriers are exposed died in large numbers. Cataract formations seem similarly related to radio exposure. Dr Pearce Bailey, in 1958, showed a congressional subcommittee that monkeys could be killed in ten to fifteen seconds with radio energy of such minute amounts that no heat induction was detectable in the experimental animals. Radio energy in the microwave range has marked chromosomal and genetic effects at very low intensities. Those of you concerned with the environment must soon face up to the problem of man-made radio energy as a toxic factor.

Let us now turn to light. Our terrestrial environment includes light coming predominantly from the sun and, in the nocturnal hours, from artificial sources. Photons, bundles of light energy, by photosynthesis in plant life are stored in vegetable products. Such products are the base energy source for human physical existence. The flow of light, as previously mentioned, can be affected by gravity. It is also affected by magnetic fields which cause the polarization axis of light to rotate. This is the so-called Faraday effect. Electrostatic fields, on the other hand, rotate the axis of polarization by way of the Kerr effect. The ancient Minoan culture of some 3,500 years ago was aware of the polarized qualities of light to the degree that their pottery was esoterically inscribed and revealed its identity only in certain polarizations which occurred at precise times of the day. As all physicists know, photons of light can be absorbed into various atomic structures with the associated displacement of the outer orbiting electrons.

We have now briefly reviewed how the atomic structures may be affected by various fields. Throughout all physical existence there is a constant interchange of these effects with one another. Much advantage is taken of these relationships in modern electronic equipment which provides us with radio and television as well as air conditioning, stoves and computers.

A significant and relatively new research tool derives from the behaviour of sub-atomic particles as spinning masses. Electron spin resonance is common language to the physicist. Seemingly the electron, spinning while orbiting within the atomic anatomy, is somewhat similar to our earth rotating while orbiting our revolving sun. Radio energy (electromagnetic waves) applied to substances at proper frequencies causes the electrons to resonate. The frequency at which resonance occurs is also dependent upon the magnetic field strength. This phenomenon is called electron paramagnetic resonance, or E.P.R. Thus all electrons are not the same; they may be spinning faster or slower and resonating at different frequencies or switching orbits with the associated absorption or emission of light energy – photons. Nobel Laureate Professor Albert Szent-Györgyi, using electron spin laboratory devices, revealed the biological work functions of electron transfer: 'The fuel of life is the electron or, more exactly, the energy it takes over from photons in photosynthesis; this energy the electron gives up gradually while flowing through the cellular machinery.'[11]

Now this accumulation of photons (light energy is heat if that energy is in the infrared range) is responsible in part for the functioning milieu of energy fields within which all cellular systems operate. The cellular light environment is not totally generated from within the cellular machinery; on the contrary, light from exterior environments penetrates deeply to within biological systems. Physicians can observe this penetration of light, in reverse fashion, by noting the luminescence on the surface of the abdomen with endoscopic instruments – such as gastroscopes. One may well postulate that certain mental characteristics are related therefore to the internal light environment of human systems provided by the light filtering effects on the skin. The redhead with his temper and the apparent differences in rote versus abstract intelligence (observed by psychologists in balanced statistical evaluations) of negroes, American Indians and caucasians can well be correlated to this skin filtering effect on light passing from the exterior to the internal cellular milieu.

Physicians associated with vascular medicine have long used infrared light thermography as a tool in evaluating vascular blood flow. That such light might also relate to mind function is suggested by one observation recorded in a sophisticated research laboratory and reported to me by cardiologist Dr Edwin Boyle. He observed that one internationally known psychic, Helen Stalls, upon initiating a psychic mode of function instantaneously exhibited a completely changed thermographic picture of the head and face.

Life fields in conjunction with other terrestrial fields combine solid, liquid and gaseous chemicals into complex sensory organisms. They do more. Life forces, Nature's alchemists, subtly transmute elements.

Albrecht von Herzeele wrote *The Origin of Inorganic Substances* one hundred years ago (1873), after observing that living plants grown in distilled water created potash, phosphorus, magnesium, calcium and sulphur. His plants seemed able to transmute phosphorus into sulphur, calcium into phosphorus, magnesium into calcium and nitrogen into potassium.

Professor Pierre Baranger, Director of the Laboratory of Organic Chemistry of the École Polytechnique in Paris, confirmed such alchemical life processes and noted their relationship to light and moon phasing. His language reveals the man:

I have been teaching chemistry at the École Polytechnique for twenty years, and believe me, the laboratory which I direct is no den of false science. But I have never confused respect for science with the taboos imposed by intellectual conformism. For me, any meticulously performed experiment is homage to science even if it shocks our ingrained habits. Von Herzeele's experiments were too few to be absolutely convincing. But their results inspired me to control them with all the precaution possible in a modern lab and to repeat them enough times so that they should be statistically irrefutable. That's what I've done.[12]

Others have shown that bacteria can turn sodium into potash and that chickens readily transmute silicon (mica) into calcium.

Science, we see, has shown that matter from the sub-atomic particle on through its organization into complex biological systems, including man, is subject to field effects of gravity, sound, magnetism, electrostatics, light and life. Science further has shown there is an interplay of these effects upon each other and that they cannot be separated from each other. Furthermore, science has observationally detected that fields of this variety can – and do – affect the highest of biological functions, that of human cognition.

The Resistance to New Ideas and Information: Pilots and Planes
Because certain men in critical occupations, such as piloting aircraft, require the highest degree of mental capabilities, one certainly has the responsibility of providing light and electrical environments conducive to increased mental activity. Pure air is not the only environmental requirement for effective human work.

Just how the mind operates is surely life's greatest mystery; but that certain electrical forces do affect mind function is well known. Possibly the most critical of human discriminations are the product of a 'higher sense perception,' some intuitive or E.S.P. sense. Recent work by Dr William Gray Walter of the Burden Neurological Institute in England demonstrated characteristic brain activity accompanying decision-making. In fact, via computer linking, he turned a T.V. set off and on without moving a muscle. Then the British Aircraft Corporation ran similar experiments using navigators, and found that navigators made decisions ten seconds before panel instruments portrayed the data requiring those decisions. In E.S.P. this would be called precognition – that is, knowing ahead of time.

A tantalizing corollary may be extracted from the work of an earlier E.S.P. researcher. Andrija Puharich, in the nineteen-fifties, had subjects in Faraday cages sending mental E.S.P. signals over a distance of a few miles. He then put positive electrostatic fields back inside these cages and found E.S.P. transmission improved by over ten times. Mother Nature has such a positive field in outdoor environments for all of us. Some very intelligent German scientists once worked for the Luftwaffe, and they put positive field devices in World War Two bombers, calling them anti-fatigue devices. About twenty years later, studies reported by Baron of the Lockheed Aircraft Corporation showed that positive electrostatic fields plus negative ion air environments improved brightness discrimination of test pilots by over ten times. At present, no American aircraft has such a device on board.

A and B, B and A

We have seen how light from the exterior penetrates to the interior of human systems, but how are electrical influences carried from the exterior to the interior of human systems, and vice versa? An examination of the *modus operandi* of acupuncture seems to give the answer to this question. Acupuncture points may be electrically detected on the surface of the skin with high-impedance volt meters. Stanford physicists Dr William Tiller and David Boyer, Thelma Moss of U.C.L.A., and I myself have confirmed prior Russian research showing that environmental versus human electrical exchanges occur at these Chinese acupuncture points. Environmental ions, which you will remember are modulated by both magnetic and electrostatic fields, are constantly exchanging with cold electron emissions from the body at acupuncture points. The forces related to these exchanges come from both terrestrial magnetic and electrostatic fields and from similar fields created by the electrical functioning of biological cellular systems. Effective acupuncture therapy modifies electrical biological energy fields and seemingly thereby relieves pain. Bodily electrical field measurements before and after relief of pain with acupuncture suggest that perception of pain may be simply the mind's cognition of abnormal electrical fields.

Now in science, when any force such as 'A' affects another force such as 'B', then we likewise see that 'B' can affect 'A'. We have pointed this out in terms of magnetics versus electrostatics and electrostatics versus magnetics, for instance. We have at this juncture pointed out how certain physical field factors affect mentality, and if our proposition is sound we should also see that mental factors affect both fields and material objects. And so it is.

Contemporarily, exciting research work is being done at Stanford University by Dr H. E. Puthoff and Dr Russell Targ with certain psychics, including Ingo Swann and Uri Geller, wherein metallic objects are bent and deformed under the influence of mind power and laser beams are deflected by thought energy alone. Curiously, it has been reported that these experiments are sometimes associated with losses of complete portions of hardware – wire and other fragments of the physical apparatus.

Recent scientific observations have confirmed that this relationship also holds with plants. Thought fields do affect plant matter. Marcel Vogel recently presented his own scientific observations on thought energy, producing predictable results on strip chart recorders which were appropriately wired to domesticated plants. Like the psychics mentioned earlier, distance appears to be no barrier to the influence of mind upon plant matter. This work, originally done by Cleve Backster in the United States and by V. N. Pushkin in the U.S.S.R., has been confirmed and greatly extended by Marcel Vogel in California.

Is thought pollution also to become an environmentalist's enigma?

Let us turn to the hard sciences; then we shall see that its conceptual problems both parallel and illuminate those of the psyche. Albert Einstein, at the turn of the century, wrote:

> It appears to me, in fact, that the observations on 'black-body radiation,' photoluminescence, the generating of cathode rays (electrons) with ultraviolet radiation, and other groups of phenomena related to the generation and transformation of light can be understood better on the assumption that the energy in light is distributed discontinuously in space. According to the presently proposed assumption the energy in a beam of light emanating from a point source is not distributed continuously over larger and larger volumes of space but consists of a finite number of energy quanta, localized at points of space, which move without subdividing and which are absorbed and emitted only as units.[13]

Einstein was concerned because in this 'black-body radiation' photons under certain conditions of encountering other photons (namely those 180 degrees off phase) simply disappeared. Jagadis Chandra Bose, an Indian physicist, submitted to Einstein a short article on 'Planck's Law and the Hypothesis of Light Quanta' from which it became apparent that larger particles, such as electrons and even gas molecules, behave similarly to the disappearing photons. Thus does hard science demonstrate that both mass and energy can simultaneously disappear.

Should we then be greatly surprised at the demonstration of similar phenomena under psychic influences? When 'A' can affect 'B', then 'B' can affect 'A', remember?

This discussion has dealt with scientific observations of the mind – of the psyche if you will. It has pointed out that mind has demonstrable external field properties recordable with field-sensitive devices. The psyche has been shown both to affect and be affected by man via incarnational and reincarnational phenomena. Similarly, the mind has been shown to affect and be affected by fields, matter, other life forms and perhaps other thought fields.

Einstein showed that in order for man to comprehend science's smaller particle, the light photon, he must look to the heavens' largest bodies – for example, our sun. Then, and only then, does Mother Nature reveal herself. With man it cannot be otherwise. He is to be discerned in the actions of the heavens which demonstrably govern his illnesses and joys, ticking inexorably the metronome of his successes and failures. Yet, without infinitely small life-supporting particles, photons and ions, no bodily system could exist.

When an examination of factual observations progresses to a sufficiently broadened vision, man's awareness – his mind or his psyche if you will – is seen, like the photon or electron of Einstein, to dance timelessly between states of being and non-being. Yet the soul persists!

One of Einstein's great friends was the Indian physicist and botanist who described the nervous systems of plants and observed their growth magnified ten million times with the crescograph which he invented. Jagadis Chandra Bose, surely one of the world's most profound thinkers, summed up his scientific philosophy thus:

> In my investigations of the action of forces on matter, I was amazed to find the boundary lines vanishing and to discover points of contact emerging between the Living and the non-Living. My first work in the region of invisible lights made me realize how in the midst of a luminous ocean we stood almost blind. Just as in following light from visible to invisible our range of investigation transcends our physical sight, so also the problem of the Great Mystery of Life and Death is brought a little nearer solution when, in the realm of the Living, we pass from the Voiced to the Unvoiced.[14]

One of the other extensively explored themes during the May Lectures was 'communication' between and among living things. This, in some sense, is an aspect of the 'interconnectedness' of living things, but because it was the subject of so much discussion it is treated separately.

Communications Between and Among Living Things
Konrad Lorenz, ethologist, recent Nobel Prize winner and

author of *On Aggression*[15] among other works, tells of a duckling that decided that he was its parent. It apparently followed him wherever he went in the same manner that it would otherwise attach itself to its natural parent. For Lorenz, this was evidence of instinctual, as opposed to learned, behaviour. But it was also evidence that some form of communication occurred between duckling and human.

It is, of course, accepted that non-verbal communication among humans exists. There has been a spate of books and articles on the subject in recent years. But it is not yet generally accepted that non-verbal communication can take place outside of sight. There is evidence available, however, to support the argument that 'lower' life forms can communicate at some distance. John Bliebtrau, in his book *The Parable of the Beast,*[16] recounts instances of this behaviour among bees. The conference at the May Lectures generally found little difficulty with the notion that non-verbal communication is possible at a distance. But they took the issue a rather large step forward. Two central questions framed the discussion. First, is it possible that some form of communication takes place at the cellular level between and among 'living' things? And second, is it possible that plants 'communicate' with one another and, as well, react to human thought projection? These are not your everyday, run-of-the-mill questions. But they were seriously addressed, with mixed results.

Cleve Backster, by training a polygraph expert, led off. Cleve dealt with both questions in a practical account of his own research.

DO PLANTS THINK?

Cleve Backster

The book *The Secret Life of Plants* has now been on best seller lists for eight weeks; a film based on the book is already under way. We are being filmed here tonight. Plant research is beginning to arouse the widest public interest.

I have always involved people directly in what I am doing. That way they are forced to take a share in the credit and the discredit. Mark Twain once said, 'There is something fascinating about science. One gets such wholesale return of conjecture out of such trifling investment of facts.' I endorse that. The Nobel Prize winner Max Planck said, 'A new scientific truth does not triumph by convincing its opponents and making them see the light, but rather because its opponents eventually die and a new generation grows up that is familiar with it.'

For the last eight years I have exposed myself as often as possible to the scientific community in the United States. Each time I speak to scientists, I remind them that I, as a scientist, am quite aware of what science and technology are about. On the other hand, I also address the general public. I walk a tight-rope between the scientist and the individual. With this precarious interface, I have to keep the respect of the former without becoming a bore to the latter. May I risk becoming just that for a moment, however, by pointing out to you that an observation is not an experiment. I have made hundreds of observations, but I have published only one experiment. Of course, even a series of published experiments does not necessarily constitute proof, until and unless that work is independently repeated. Although an investigator can privately think that 'proof' exists, more than that is required before a change will or can occur in the thinking of scientists in general.

There are essentially two roles in science – the theorist and the experimentalist. I attribute my presence here to having resisted the temptation to explain my observations. You can get into serious difficulty if you try to explain something before you are ready. Good, reliable data may be ignored by the scientific community simply on the basis of faulty explanation. But I have never allowed what I call the 'authoritarian reject' to interfere with my work. The 'authoritarian reject' operates when someone who is, or thinks he is, an authority shouts 'Nonsense!' And you immediately stop what you are doing.

My first encounter with plant life as a researcher was in February 1966. Then I assumed that if a plant could respond to a stimulus, the response would occur at the 'whole' plant level. Later I found that a plant leaf detached from the plant, or even a piece of a leaf cut to the size of the electrodes, could be successfully used in my research. Moreover, a pulverized leaf smeared on the electrodes was likewise effective. These observations strongly suggested that the plant response phenomenon occurred at the cell cluster level. Since then my research has descended the evolutionary scale still further. I am now working with single-celled organisms, both flora and bacteria. In your breakfast yoghourt, for example, there are millions of sentient creatures. My findings may be bad news for vegetarians. Unless vegetables and other 'lowly' life forms are cheerfully, sacrificing their lives in order to be eaten by you, one of the fundamental arguments against meat-eating – the consumption of tissue once alive like us – is dissolved.

We have also focused on single-celled organisms such as unfertilized chicken eggs. And we are also working with cells in vitro – that is, cell samples removed from a donor. Our preliminary indications are that these cells, once divided into groups, can 'communicate' with each other, even though physically separated. This observation, if confirmed, has some fairly profound implications for biology and medicine.*
Under present theory, we would not even argue that cells can communicate while in the body, except through the neural or chemical messenger systems. We are faced with many questions.

The Experiments

Among the equipment we work with is the lie-detector. (My professional involvement over the last twenty-five years has been as a polygraph expert. In that field, at least, I have preserved my respectability.) I make my forays into other disciplines – biology, zoology and so forth – as a polygraph expert. The lie-detector or any other piece of conventional

* One of the implications is very startling – when a person thinks harmful thoughts about some of his own cells in vitro, the cells violently react. This finding implies – as has been rumoured by many different disciplines in the past – that when you think bad thoughts about yourself you are not being just conceptually negative, but may actually be adversely affecting the cells in your body.

polygraph equipment has a number of pens registering events from different parts of the organism. One may record breathing rhythm, another activity in the stomach area, a third changes in blood pressure, a fourth pulse rate, and so on. Of particular interest is the galvanic skin response, from which we infer psychological reactions on the part of the individual under examination, through the 'response' reflected in changes in the electrical conductivity of the skin. Through the use of these measures, the polygraph records when the subject is, for instance, lying or prevaricating. A similar reaction occurs when a threat is made to an individual's well-being – if he is threatened with a prison sentence, for example, either literally or by inference. The upward swing and recovery of the graph that we observe in those cases is the most significant for our present purposes. This same swing can be observed in the polygraph records obtained from plants when the life or well-being of that plant is threatened. I first saw such a curve produced by a plant on February 2nd, 1966 (Figure 4).

The first plant I worked with was a Dracena cane plant. The Dracena had been around the laboratory for some time. I had no particular interest in these plants, or for that matter in plants in general. They were not connected with my research. For the previous eight years I laboured for the Research and Instrument Committee of the American Polygraph Association. On February 2nd, 1966, I had been working all night. Around 7.30 a.m. I was enjoying a coffee break. Just to relax, I watered the plants. I wondered how long it took water to reach the leaves of a plant. After the watering, I crudely attached two electrodes to the plant leaf with a rubber band. I expected, if anything, to see a slow, upward curve on the graph – denoting that the water was finally reaching the leaf with the result of lowering its electrical resistance. I found, however, that the tracing was tending downward. I adjusted the pen upward slightly, but again the graph trend was down. After about a minute more I had just about abandoned the idea that this was a useful way to examine the diffusion of moisture through a plant – although the thought did occur to me that the downward drift of the graph mapped what polygraph operators see after

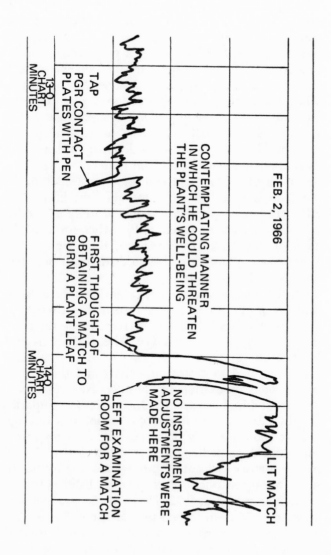

FIG. 4   SECTION OF THE FEBRUARY 2, 1966 PLANT MONITORING CHART
SHOWING THE REACTION WHICH OCCURRED AT THE SAME TIME THAT
THE AUTHOR THOUGHT OF BURNING THE PLANT LEAF.

a human being is first connected to the machine and his initial anxiety is dissipated.

Then I noticed an upward swing of the pen, reminiscent of the typical anxiety reaction of a human being. Perhaps I could induce 'anxiety' in a plant. My mind was already buzzing with queries – how can a plant display reactions, and so on. So I tried dipping a plant leaf in hot coffee. No reaction. Then I inspected the machine for possible mechanical defects and found none. So I again considered what might constitute a threat to a plant's well-being. At that moment the thought of fire entered my head, along with the intent to actually burn the plant. The polygraph pen shot off the top of the record paper and a burst of wild oscillations followed. I had no matches. I was two or three feet from the equipment and some ten feet from the plant. I concluded, therefore, that my thought had produced the effect. In later experiments, when we only pretended to burn the plant, we got no reaction. But when we 'really' intend to, as I did on that first occasion, then we get a reaction. Presumably, plants are able to distinguish between our real and feigned intentions.

After the first plant response, I went next door and took some matches from a desk. As I returned with the matches, I changed my mind. I decided to remove the threat. I returned the matches to the next office. The oscillations immediately levelled off.

I was tempted to destroy the chart and forget it. I had my professional reputation to consider. Nevertheless, I realized that what I had apparently discovered was important. What should I do? Obviously, I could not run out into Times Square shouting, 'My plant has just read my mind!' Prostitutes and dope-pedlars are given latitude in the area where my laboratory is located, but I knew the authorities would scoop me up at once. Consequently, I did nothing until my colleague arrived at 9.15. He eyed me strangely – as a rule I would have been in bed by that time. I requested that he ask me no questions, but rather go into the laboratory, hook the electrodes to the plant and see what results, if any, he could obtain. He obtained results very similar to those I had observed.

Next, we decided to find out if the cane plant might have been unusual. Accordingly, we started to work with about thirty-five different varieties of plant life. And we changed the polygraph equipment several times. Still later we tested plants in other geographical locations, to be sure that we were not arousing purely local phenomena – eventually I tested plants in the Middle East. Finally, we tested plants growing under natural conditions, as well as in the laboratory. Wherever and however we tested, our results confirmed our original finding.

My next step was to contact different people in the New York scientific community, from a variety of disciplines. I stressed that I was not interested in wild speculation. No doubt, I said, there is some obvious explanation, and I would be grateful if they could tell me what it was. I contacted a chemist, a botanist, a zoologist, a psychologist – even a psychiatrist! They were unable to reach any conclusion. Before each observer left, I asked whether he could suggest any controls which should be integrated into further experimentation.

Thereafter, we consumed many, many hours in pure observation. We did not conduct specific experiments, but merely hooked the plants to the polygraph and continued with our regular work. But we maintained a record which reflected when the plants appeared to respond to something, so we could relate the responses to external events. Later we added a tone device, so that sudden rises in pitch alerted us instantly to significant responses.

Many of our subsequent observations were stimulating. We observed that a plant appeared to regard a not easily defined area as its territory. The plant might respond in any room on the floor where the laboratory was, but not to stimuli from a building adjacent to the laboratory and literally closer geographically. An event occurring only ten feet away might not register, while one seventy feet away would. There did not appear to be any progression of effects as one might expect from our knowledge of the electromagnetic spectrum. Certainly things that could harm plant life occur all the time. A plant, however, appears to be only 'attuned' to events taking place in its own relevant 'environment'. We also found that plants seemed to develop an 'attachment' to their caretakers. Events in the caretakers' lives seemed to blanket out other stimuli. We monitored some caretakers up to thirty miles away from their plants – their emotional stresses were faithfully recorded by the plants. In addition, we did some further investigation at longer distances. We noted, for example, that some plants recorded responses precisely at the moment of touch-down of an aeroplane bearing its owner hundreds of miles away. 'Touchdown' is, of course, frequently a time of high anxiety, even for the most seasoned traveller.

The plants were also attuned to other life-forms in the laboratory. On one occasion I dumped some scalding water into the sink. The pen of the polygraph twenty-five feet away immediately went right off the chart. The plant had possibly reacted to the scalding of the bacteria in the sink. There was no reaction with a sterile sink.

Once I took some yoghourt from the refrigerator in the laboratory. The yoghourt was the kind that has jam in the bottom that you stir in. When I began to stir in the jam, the tone generator attached to the polygraph equipment quickly loudened. Ostensibly, some chemical in the jam kills the live bacteria in the yoghourt on contact. The plant again seemed to react to the death of some life-form.

A Spider at Yale

Plants seem particularly attuned to insects. At first I found it difficult to get a public platform for this revelation. Then I received an invitation from the Yale Linguistics Club to talk on non-verbal communication. By the time they found out what I was really up to, it was too late! Following the particular lecture, I adjourned with some graduates and staff to another room where I brought out my polygraph. Having shown those present how to adjust the various knobs, I let them take over. Someone brought in an ivy leaf and attached it to the machine. I then suggested that we looked for an insect, and a spider was soon found. Whenever a student frustrated the spider from moving, the spider would first freeze and then would suddenly run. The split second before it ran, the pen of the polygraph would give a violent jerk.

This occurred five or six times in a row. Then we conceived the idea of letting the spider run down the staircase. One student hunted it, while another called out the readings on the machine chart. Even when the hunter could not see the spider, if the machine reflected a strong reaction, he was always close to it. Soon thereafter he would actually find it.

The Power of Positive Thinking

A plant physiologist once visited me at the University of Ottawa. She told me of some work she had been doing to expedite plant growth by sound bombardment and asked me to demonstrate some of my findings for her. I fetched and connected up one, two, three, four, five plants – and got no reactions. Then I asked her what she did; whether her work harmed plants. She replied that she put them in ovens and roasted them to obtain their dry weight! We speak of dogs being able to detect people hostile to animals. I think my plants spotted this woman in the same kind of way – they had fainted. After she left for the airport, I reconnected the same plants and observed the recordings reflecting a kind of free oscillating movement – a form of joyous dance, perhaps? Many people have been talking to their plants for years – in secret. Our observations suggest that those people who feel sorry for their plants when they go away on holiday, and who generally consider plants to be alive and receptive, are the same people we often refer to as having green fingers. I have also noted that people, when persuaded to alter their attitude to plants, begin to have greater success in growing and maintaining them. The difference between being able and not being able to grow plants may lie in our attitude to plants. Recently, I have suggested to people that they think positively about their plants when they are away – perhaps even look at a photograph of them once or twice a day. Since distance apparently may have little or no effect on the affective bond, this step may prevent the deterioration or death of plants left unattended. The early reports we have had are encouraging.

The Experiment

We were eager to disseminate our results, but prior to

approaching the general public we needed one water-tight, controlled experiment. We decided upon an experiment involving brine-shrimps. The shrimps were to be dumped into boiling water while the plant was connected to recording equipment at the other end of the laboratory. Unfortunately, we ran into all kinds of problems. The experiment did not work properly while we were in the laboratory. Moreover, it did not help if we left the laboratory. The plant had still had a chance to attune to us. Ultimately, one individual fetched a plant and another fetched the shrimps (and both were kept out of the laboratory until the last minute); then we rushed in and connected the plant up to the experimental apparatus. Thereafter, the experiment proceeded by pre-programmed and randomized remote control.

A few further details about the set-up. We built our own equipment because we had no funds to purchase it. We constructed a randomly programmed electrical circuit which made and broke the connections. The tilting of the brine cup, for example, broke the connection, which was renewed only when the cup was back in place. We had thermostats holding the water in the immersion bath at a constant temperature and an agitating paddle to prevent the build-up of cool spots. We even had a fan blowing air under the cup containing the shrimps so that rising steam could not give them any hint of their imminent demise. Still, we had problems with the shrimps. If they were not healthy, the plant would display no reaction. This finding raises some interesting philosophical questions, however. The practical problem was how to decide whether a batch of shrimps were healthy or not. Biology came to our rescue. Brine-shrimps are very interested in perpetuating their species. A healthy shrimp is either engaged in sex or manoeuvring to become so engaged. So we placed pairs of males and females in the cup and observed. Those that vigorously pursued each other were used in the experiment.

Our randomization techniques proved to be important. If we, as investigators, knew in advance when an immersion was to occur, that knowledge could interfere with the plant reaction – even override the reaction to the immersion of the shrimp. Finally, in addition to the three polygraphs attached to three separate plants, a fourth polygraph remained unconnected as a control.

Under these conditions we obtained significant data and published a paper on our work in the *International Journal of Parapsychology*.[17] In the paper we shared our findings that plants will respond – in so far as polygraph records demonstrate such responses – to the death of other living matter – in this case brine-shrimps.

The Egg and I

We continue to stumble over new phenomena. I kept a Dobermann pinscher in the laboratory and fed him an egg a day to keep his coat healthy. One day I broke the egg as usual to feed the dog, and the polygraph went wild. I was surprised – the egg was not fertile; it had been purchased from a supermarket around the corner. The next day I watched more carefully, and the polygraph recorded a reaction the instant I broke the egg. I then worked out a way to attach polygraph electrodes to an egg shell. I boiled small sponges in salt water and placed these between the electrodes and the shell. Then I ran a recording of the egg for nine hours. Among other items, I obtained a cyclic rate of oscillation appropriate to a chick egg approximately $3\frac{1}{2}$ to 4 days in incubation. Yet, on opening up the egg and performing an embryology, no trace of any physical structure was found. We have not been able to repeat this experiment under controlled conditions, but we have had the same observation a number of times – our graph records show the rhythms of a developing heart, but in a non-fertile egg. This result suggests that some etheric force field or blueprint exists before a corresponding physical organ develops. Perhaps the physical event is preceded by – or in some sense caused by – a previously existing blueprint of a non-physical nature?

We have also recorded eggs 'reacting' to their environment. I discovered that eggs react to the 'death' of another egg. I rigged a device that would transfer eggs into boiling fat in a random sequence. Another egg, attached to electrodes, produced a 'fainting' response when the egg hit the fat.

Other Bizarre Events

I have also observed reactions from one container of yoghourt to interference with another container. It even happens when I remember what I have done to the first yoghourt. This finding has some interesting implications for biological research – a researcher might be interfering with what is happening in an experiment, without being aware of that fact.

As a double-X rated example, I have also worked with human sperm. A sperm sample in a test tube will react to the donor, forty feet away through three closed doors, who breaks a capsule of amyl nitrite, a substance which lowers blood pressure. The fumes of the capsule hitting the donor's fingers apparently causes a reaction in the sperm. Sample sniffing and inhaling the gas produces another. This experiment can be readily repeated.

One of our major findings is that people can distinctly disturb what they are observing. If someone is extremely sceptical about an experiment, their scepticism affects the results. To test this, I use a video-tape cassette in a closed-circuit television camera. The camera records the chart, while simultaneously recording the sound in the room where I confer with visitors. Those whom I suspect of scepticism, I show first how the experiment is designed and describe its objectives. Then I suddenly add a comment such as, 'You don't suppose that bacteria could have any kind of consciousness?' The visitor usually replies that, of course, it does not. Then we play back the recording. Generally, before the visitor has actually uttered the words 'Of course not,' the pen has jumped off the chart. This is a wonderful way of opening closed minds – we show the sceptic that he or she has interacted with organisms in a controlled and monitored experiment.

What Does All This Mean?

Our research, in our view, is linked with the great expansion of consciousness many have observed. Rapid advances are now possible; a new science may be emerging.

Backster's conclusions are a little slender. But there seem to be three propositions. First, there is some evidence that plant life 'responds' to 'signals' transmitted by other plants and other living things, including human beings. Second, Backster's research, and that of others (most of which is described in *The Secret Life of Plants*[18]) suggests that there is, or are modes of, 'communication between and among living things which have not yet been identified.' Whether these 'modes' are at all related dynamically to the concepts of energy and field theory, which are raised in some of the other presentations, is unknown but conceptually possible. We may be dancing around the edges of a unifying, universal field theory, but it is far too early to argue the case convincingly. The third proposition has been discussed earlier: it is clear that an investigator's attitudes, thoughts and expectations can influence the results of an experiment. In the case of Cleve Backster, it appears that even the most tenuous thought pattern is detectable by his plants. The same phenomenon is evident in the work of Marcel Vogel, perhaps even more so.

Backster's original work provoked a number of people to either replicate or debunk. One of those who decided to find out what was going on was Marcel Vogel, Senior Chemist at I.B.M. in San Jose, California. Vogel is an engaging and energetic man. His oral presentation is almost more 'experimental' than 'substantive', which is not to say that he does not offer substantive conclusions. In his presentation Vogel traced his own immersion in plant research, one associated with much soul-searching because of the pressures of his peer group. He also used some visualization techniques which cannot be reproduced in written form. Because so much of Vogel's presentation was kinetic – and experiential – it is difficult to capture in essay form. One observer, Stan Gooch, author of *Total Man* and *Personality and Evolution,* had this to say:

Some ten minutes after the start of his lecture, Marcel Vogel announced that he was going to give us, the audience, proof of the tangible reality of thought by projecting a thought image into our hands. My instant reaction was, 'No, don't – don't attempt that.' For although no stranger to telepathy, I had never yet met anyone who could produce results to order. I felt Vogle was putting his head on the block quite unnecessarily. He then asked us to close our eyes. More in sorrow than in anger – that is to say, very half-heartedly – I did so. Vogel then announced that he was beginning the transmission of the image. In my mind's eye (and apparently somewhere around the middle of my forehead) I 'saw' at that point a triangle, on which seemed to be superimposed a rather less clear circle. I opted for the triangle. Vogel then said he was giving the image a colour. At first it seemed to me that the triangle was blue – then it became red – and I opted definitely for red. Vogel said we should now open our eyes. He asked how many of us had had an image. Some fifty people or so raised their hands. I must confess I did not bother to raise mine. Vogel pointed to one of the volunteers – 'You sir, what did you get?' The answer – a triangle. At this point I almost literally fell off my seat. Further shock was already on its way. Vogel told us that he had projected the image of a triangle enclosed in a circle. First he had coloured it yellow, but then after a moment had switched the colour to red. I spent the rest of that lecture in what I can only describe as a state of joy. At the close the audience clapped enthusiastically. But why did they only clap? We should have stamped and shouted and broken the chairs in honour of this world-beater.

INTERPERSONAL COMMUNICATION BETWEEN MAN AND PLANT

Marcel Vogel, M.Sc.

Why and how does a plant respond to a human thought or emotion? In 1905, Jagadis Chandra Bose established that there is in fact a nervous system in plants. He believed that plants were capable of experiencing sensory responses by precisely the same mechanisms as human beings. He sectioned the stem of a plant and found cells that were identical in staining to the nerve cells of humans. He applied electrical stimuli to the section and found in fact a faster response to the stimulus than in humans. He found that he could anaesthetize the response with chloroform and ether. He found that a plant could be killed with poisons such as strychnine and potassium cyanide. He measured the death spasms of mimosa. In all, he published twelve enormous volumes of research. There is scarcely a mention of these in any American or British publication. It is one of the crimes of this century that his work has been entirely neglected.

In Santa Rosa, California, the plant expert Luther Burbank found that when he focused his attention on a plant, he was able to cause that plant to take the shape he desired. That was in 1900. From Burbank we can track back further to Charles Darwin. Darwin was interested in the movement of plants. He has written about how the root of a plant is like the mind of man – it directs activity, selects and makes the decisions that are necessary for the outer life-form to be maintained. He made an intensive study of insectivorous plants and found much the same reactions as Bose – that a plant can be overstimulated and worked too hard. It would reject certain types of food in favour of others. He also concluded that something very suspiciously like intelligence operates in plants. However, these aspects of Darwin's work have been ignored. Yet there is intelligence in every living cell on this planet. It is called cellular consciousness. It is that which maintains the form of the cell. And there is inter-communication between cells – that knowledge we owe to the Russians.

I was in Prague last year, taking part in the first international conference on paraphysics and parapsychology. Subsequently, I was invited to Moscow University and spoke there to Pushkin and Dr Pressman. They showed me some experiments they were performing to study intercellular communication. In each of two Petri dishes of quartz they placed some human tissue cells. Then the two plates were stacked one on top of the other. Poison was put in the top dish, and then it was closed. At the moment the cells in the top dish died, those in the bottom dish also died. When pyrex dishes that would not pass short-wave ultraviolet were substituted for the quartz dishes, the effect did not occur.

Gerwich predicted back in 1920 that there was a microgenetic radiation emitted or radiated from living cells and that this radiation was a means of communication between one cell and another. We do generate a field at the cellular level. We generate composite fields at the mental level and the most powerful, potent force at the highest conscious levels. Christ said if we have faith great enough we can move mountains. I have seen physical objects moved by the power of the mind.*

How to Communicate

Both at the cellular and the macrostructural level, then, there are in the plant forms of consciousness and awareness. There is also an etheric body to a plant, and I will tell you how to communicate with it. You do so by interacting with the plant field with your hand held at a critical distance. Then you move your hand back and forth. As you 'cut' across the field you will then feel a charge building up in your hand. When there is a balance of charge between your hand and the leaf, you start oscillating your hand this way and that. The leaf will begin to move up and away again, interacting with your hand.

This is the first level of communication. If this is done, a bond is established – a field or force bond. This is a channel of communication. The link I am discussing here has not been discussed in any publication to date. You first have to interact with the plant before anything further can happen. The plant does not generate intelligence of its own. It is necessary for you to get your intelligence 'into' the plant; you write the programme in your head and impart it to the plant. If you do not 'write it', nothing happens.

Monitoring the Plant

We connect up the plant to our polygraph by a pair of stainless steel electrodes attached to the sides of a leaf. The

---

* In paranormal research terms, this is referred to as psychokinesis.

leads are fed through some minor pieces of equipment, including a Wheatstone bridge, to the strip chart recorder. When we first attach the plant, we observe a series of wild oscillations on the graph paper. This is because the plant is sensitive to light and all the other forces around you. You balance the bridge, but the signal drifts off again. Then you focus your mind on the plant. The signal drifts more slowly and then suddenly you have it under control. There is no longer any apparent responsiveness to light or electrostatic charges, except through your mind. Then, by releasing a thought, a reaction occurs. Or you can release emotion and get a different reaction. Or you might meditate and see what is produced. You can unfold a map of many of your different states of mind.

The Plant Responses

When I approach a plant experimentally, I begin by giving it bursts of love – a kind of affirmation of growth. The result is a shift in the permanent base-line of the chart. I am five feet or so away from the plant at the time. I do this two or three times, on each occasion creating a new base-line, until there is a kind of maximal locking-in of the effect, and then I stop. The plant has been boosted, and I am in communication with it.

Numerous charts show the effect of various thoughts on the plant, in terms of sudden oscillations from the base-line Thoughts included such matters as tearing a leaf, breaking a leaf off completely and burning a leaf. The responses to thoughts are often very rapid, in the millisecond range in fact. This is the reaction time of the plant. The oscillation then continues for as long as the thought is held. What is of very considerable importance is that the actual act of burning or tearing leaves causes no reaction on the graph. It is the thought of doing damage which produces the response, and only the thought.

When one becomes fully attuned to a plant, a rhythmic oscillation takes place. It is a pulse beat of the interaction between man and plant. The oscillation occurs, as I have discovered, when one is giving a truly intense form of love or interaction. I have further found that when a psychic healer is doing a healing, if they are simultaneously linked into a plant, the same rhythmic oscillation is observed. Every individual's oscillation is distinct and personal. I have conducted monitoring experiments with healers in close proximity and at considerable distances. When the link is established, despite the distance, the pulse beat occurs.

The work of Backster and Vogel is both different and alike. Backster recognizes the influence of the investigator and thus takes steps, such as using automated equipment, to remove or at least nullify investigator bias. Also, Backster appears to be much more interested in the pure 'response' of the plant dissociated from his expectations, or 'thought projections' to use Vogel's phrase. Vogel, on the other hand, conducts his experiments as if to test the plants' responses to his responses to various stimuli. He seems less concerned with plant response to various stimuli than with his 'interpersonal' interaction with the plant. But despite these differences in experimental design, both investigators are at work on a frontier of science. Some have criticized their work as 'pseudo-science'. Both men are sensitive to this criticism and have taken steps to purify their experimental designs. In any event, their work continues, and others stimulated by their efforts will no doubt begin to look at some of the same questions.

One of the more provocative issues in plant communication research is what the 'medium' is for the transmission of communication – what pathway does the communication track? This same sort of question arises in the examination of psychic healing.

The Dynamics of Healing

Radiation, or Kirlian photography, is in its infancy. In simple terms, through the use of this process, body fields can be 'photographed'. Radiation photography does not 'prove' anything. It seems clear that the human body is surrounded by a 'field', but we do not fully appreciate its significance. But at a minimum, the existence of the 'field' gives us something new to work with in searching for health. The most up-to-date work on the 'Kirlian' process has been done by Dennis Milner at the University of Birmingham. In his book entitled *The Loom of Creation*, soon to be published, Milner reveals some of the most striking photographic displays. The photographs in the book show dancing and provocative patterns of 'energy' or 'life' fields; it is not clear what to call them. Sensitive to criticism of previous Kirlian work, Milner developed practical processes which were invulnerable to known sources which could have imprinted the film. The only conclusion, then, according to Milner, is that energy fields must exist, about which we know little, and these may be responsible for 'organizing' much of our life experiences.

The existence of the 'Kirlian effect' does not repudiate allopathic theory, but is evidence that there is a new phenomenon – the energy field – which might serve as an indicator for use in diagnosis and healing.[19] There are healers who base their practices on body field or 'aura' readings.[20] Some healers claim that a person's aura or field alters with the presence of disease, and that therapy has as its purpose the restoration of the natural field. The data then only illustrates that a variety of approaches can be taken to healing. Allopathic medicine has 'selected' only some phenomena for investigation and, correspondingly, its vision and tools are limited. There are other ways.

The claims of healers have been supported by a substantial number of people, including some who have not personally experienced a healing. But despite wide-spread support, psychic or faith healing has been severely handicapped by two problems: its association with religious expression and activity and the lack of any material proof of its efficacy.

The first handicap is slowly being overcome by the dissociation of many healers from conventional religious dogma and, somewhat paradoxically, at the same time by an affirmation of spirituality stripped of dogma. The second problem is somewhat disingenuous. Modern medicine lacks 'proof' for the bulk of its procedures and processes. There is little evidence available to link many of the procedures customarily used in medicine to the outcomes of patients.

Nevertheless, the charge is true – aside from the claims of healers and the healed, unconventional healing has lacked an empirical base. This was the problem that bothered Justa Smith.

BIOENERGETICS IN HEALING
Dr Sister Justa Smith

The basis for discussing new approaches to health and healing is the notion of energy exchange. This energy, however, is so subtle that in spite of our advanced technology we lack instruments to measure it. Hence we may be investigating wavelengths lying at extreme ends of the electromagnetic spectrum, or these new 'energies' may not be part of the electromagnetic spectrum. Perhaps 'energies' is not the word we should be using. Wholly new vocabularies may be needed for these new phenomena. What is certain is that we have no way of measuring or describing the 'energy' to which the illness or malfunction of organisms and organic material responds so positively.

Until recently, we have been held back by science itself. Scientists have been unwilling to acknowledge the possible existence of events for which there are no known parameters, no theoretical basis of explanation – which seem to lie beyond the laws of chemistry and physics. Little by little, however, scientists are becoming aware that phenomena exist which cannot be made to fit within prevailing and rigid categories. A few are now willing to admit that areas outside the conventional arena do merit investigation. That admission alone takes vision and courage.

Although representing a new field for science, the phenomena themselves are not new – in the sense that they have been a feature of the cultural and conceptual scene of 'primitive' cultures throughout history. These cultures did not feel they had to explain or understand an event before they accepted it for what it manifestly was. Only our modern, sophisticated culture refuses to acknowledge the existence of events simply on the grounds that the conceptual tools to measure them are not available.

The Human Dimensions Institute

The Human Dimensions Institute in New York has as its simple objective the understanding of man. We at the Institute maintain that the full potential and dimensions of man can only be realized in a completely normal – that is, healthy – body. We have concerned ourselves these past years with two approaches to health: one, the treatment or healing of the sick body, and two, the maintenance of good health through proper and adequate nutrition.

As a biochemist, I believe that enzymes and the balance of enzyme systems are at the root of all proper functioning of the body. Enzymes are, so to speak, the 'brains' of the individual cells which they catalyze. Without enzymes, cells undergo no radical changes. In a sense, the enzyme 'inspires' events in the cell. I believe that all healing, and all good health, must relate to metabolic interchanges between cell and enzyme. The hypothesis that enzymes are centrally involved in good health and healing, though a logical one, remains to be demonstrated.

An opportunity presented itself when I heard of the fascinating work of Dr Bernard Grad of McGill University. Dr Grad had found, through a series of carefully controlled experiments, that a healer could hasten the rates of growth and healing in mice and plants. One explanatory hypothesis is that the healer creates a field contiguous to the field surrounding the organism, and that some energy exchange between the fields may then take place. If an 'exchange' takes place, it should be detectable at an enzyme level. While Dr Grad's date is extremely convincing, I approached the possibility of a paranormal healer effecting a cure as a sceptic. No other initial approach is possible for a biochemist, since it is theoretically difficult to accept, let alone explain, that a paranormal healer can produce a true cure. Through the offices of Dr Grad, I was able to obtain the services of a healer – Mr Estebany. The hypothesis to be tested was that any healing force channelled through, or co-ordinated by, the hands of a paranormal healer must affect the activities of enzymes, if true healing is to be said to have occurred.

Mr Estebany is a man of about seventy-five years, Hungarian by birth. Like all the healers I have met, he has a quiet confidence in what he is doing. There was nothing boastful; merely a radiance of inner conviction. He and I immediately established an excellent working rapport, despite the difficulty of his sometimes quaint English.

My approach to the matters under investigation was comparative. As a result of my past work, I determined among other things to compare any effects obtained by this healer with those obtained by exposing enzymes to strong magnetic fields. The enzyme I chose for study was a proteolytic enzyme – that is, one which digests specific known proteins.

The Experiment

The experimental procedure was as follows. One large batch of enzymes in solution was prepared and divided into four equal parts. The first of these was set aside to serve as a normal control. The second batch was submitted to Mr Estebany for treatment. We asked him to do to the solution whatever he normally did when he tried to heal. So, for ninety minutes each morning, he sat quietly with his hands around the glass vessel containing the enzyme solution. Every fifteen minutes, without disturbing the healer, an assistant withdrew three millilitres of the solution by pipette. These samples were placed in identical vials, each covered with foil and with the code marked on the underside. The control solution was similarly sampled at the same time. I should add that the control solution, immersed in a bath of water, was held at constant temperature – a vital methodological consideration.

The third batch of enzyme solution was meanwhile exposed to a high magnetic field of thirteen thousand gauss, and the fourth batch was exposed to ultraviolet radiation. This last step was the result of a suggestion by Dr Grad. He pointed out that what I had demanded of Mr Estebany was analogous to asking a healer to heal a well person. There was nothing *wrong* with the enzymes that I had asked him to influence. Dr Grad suggested that I damage an enzyme preparation to see if Mr Estebany could correct the damage. I already knew that the activity levels of enzymes could be reduced by exposure to ultraviolet radiation. Therefore, in this fourth batch of enzymes, I reduced the activity of the enzymes by twenty per cent.

A word or two of additional explanation is perhaps necessary here. An enzyme is a biological catalyst – that is, it has to act on something before activity can be measured. What it acts upon we call a substrate. The substrate I used in these experiments was chromogenic. In non-technical terms, the effect of an enzyme on this substance is to cleave a bond. Further, the portion of the substance that is thereby broken away has a colour. A spectrophotometer can readily measure the quantity that has been cleaved off. This reading is then the measure of the degree of activity of the enzyme. A small amount of arithmetic would therefore show us how far Mr Estebany had succeeded in raising the activity of the fourth batch of enzyme solution, deliberately and experimentally lowered by a factor of twenty per cent.

The results

Our results show that Mr Estebany succeeding in raising the level of activity of the 'normal' enzyme solution by a statistically significant amount. This was, then, a positive and significant result.*

Next, what were the results obtained with the sample damaged by ultraviolet radiation? Mr Estebany did succeed in raising the level of activity of the damaged enzymes, though not to the hundred per cent active level. My belief is that he might have raised the level of activity fully back to normal – that is, he would have 'cured' the enzymes completely – had he been able to treat the solution over a number of days, instead of just one. A patient would be treated on several successive occasions. Unfortunately, an enzyme solution rapidly denatures itself over time – that is,

---

* A word of caution: we could not run all experiments and all parts of experiments simultaneously. We had insufficient instrumentation. While we always state the times of day of each experiment along with each set of results, repetition of this experimental series should avoid variations in time of day, if possible.

it undergoes self-generated change, so a new solution had to be used every day.

Of great interest is the fact that the results obtained from Mr Estebany's 'healing' of the first, normal batch of enzymes rather closely resemble those obtained with the solution exposed to a high magnetic field. This naturally prompts the question, is there a magnetic field effect involved in a healer's healing powers? No simple answer can be given. First, two identical or similar effects can arise from two very different causes. Second, when I attempted to measure any magnetic field effect between the hands of Mr Estebany with a very sensitive gauss meter, nothing registered. That in turn might be either because no magnetic field is involved, or because Mr Estebany in some way nullifies the operation of the meter. Psychics have had some very strange effects on laboratory equipment – as other researchers will witness.

One final technical point. It is impossible for us to make sure that the same number of molecules of solution are present in every sample, though of course we measure the amounts as precisely as possible. This constitutes a possible source of error statistically, which would be reflected in the rather large standard deviations of our results. (A standard deviation is approximately the average amount of deviation you can expect to find, by chance alone, between any of your actual results and the arithmetically computed average of all your results.) The effect of a large standard deviation is to nullify – that is, render non-significant – any apparently positive or negative results you obtain. Nevertheless, the results from the study of Mr Estebany's healing remain statistically significant.

Estebany and the Doctor

Aside from the detailed experimental work I have described, we also ran an informal study of Dr Estebany in the afternoons, when he was not required by us in the laboratory. A young physician who practised locally was interested in the phenomena of paranormal healing. The informal study was organized in the following way. The physician took Mr Estebany to his office, where he provided him with a room. The doctor referred to him those of his patients who were not suffering from any urgent medical condition and who, moreover, were willing to be seen by Mr Estebany. Mr Estebany then treated the patients in the manner and on as many separate occasions as he deemed appropriate. When he felt he had done as much for the patient as he could, the patient was returned to the doctor, who would perform an examination and arrive at a judgment.

I cannot give you a detailed account of what the doctor concluded. The results have remained locked away in the doctor's office for several years now. What I can tell you is this. Of the twenty-four patients who were seen by the healer, twenty-three said that they now felt 'much better'. Two of them were referred to a psychiatrist by Estebany after their first session with him. Only one patient reported that he felt the same. The doctor's only published reaction to his patients' new-found well-being was, apparently, 'Oh!'

The Second Set of Tests

We later ran a follow up programme. In the autumn, we had Estebany back again and ran the experimental series a second time. The environmental and background circumstances were very different. First, instead of Estebany living in the residence hall, because we were now in full session he had to live off campus. Secondly, it was a typically ugly Buffalo winter. Finally, and perhaps most important of all, Estebany was going through a severe family crisis. To cut a long story short, Estebany had no effect on the enzymes or on the patients in the second series.

You cannot imagine how devastating this was for me. I had, whatever else, made the mistake of anticipating results – something a scientist must never do – and I felt desperately disappointed. When I had calmed down sufficiently, I tried to account for what had happened. Perhaps the healer must have personal tranquillity in order to produce his effects. Physical surroundings might also play a part. At our second meeting, Estebany was not a well man himself.

There is a story which sheds some light on this point. A doctor who was by inclination a researcher had a patient with a rare and unusual condition. The physician was convinced he could devise a medicine that would help this patient. Finally he felt he had the answer. He dispatched the formula out of state to be made up. It came back and he gave the client sufficient medicine for a two-week dosage. He instructed the patient to return after this interval. On his return, the patient had progressed. At this time the doctor discontinued the medicine for a further two-week period – and the patient grew worse again. The doctor had a second batch of the formula made up, and this time he gave his patient a one-week dose. The patient improved. Finally, the physician gave his client one further week's medicine – and this time the patient deteriorated. The doctor was happy. He confessed to the patient that the final dose had been a placebo. And it had not helped, despite the patient's belief in it, thus proving that the medicine had real curative powers. The doctor wrote to the drug company, describing what had happened and claiming to have discovered a new medicine. The drug company wrote back saying, 'Sir, you are in error. We tested *you*. The whole of the second batch we sent was placebo.'

It is possibly not so important that the patient have faith in the doctor, but that the doctor have faith in himself. Perhaps Estebany did not have faith in himself during our second experiment.

All the data I have presented to you tends to support the idea of the transcendental nature of healing. These data help to confirm what many of us already suspect – that there is something, some force or energy, within the body that controls the healing processes of growth and repair. No disease has ever been cured by any practitioner of medicine. I do not believe that doctors heal. I believe that the doctor does many things to facilitate and assist the healing process, but that in the final analysis the body heals itself.

There are other ways to test the psychic component in healing. Psychic factors operate in many conventional medical practices. Too often when the phrase 'psychic healing' is used, the assumption is made that the healing is undertaken in some occultist way by a non-physician. This is not necessarily the case. There are undoubtedly many physicians who rely on psychic awareness in their practices, consciously or otherwise. There are, of course, some doctors who claim that they can perceive bodily auras and so on. But beyond these few, many other physicians probably possess psychic skills and use them in their work.

Healing is not the only arena for psychics. Since many of them claim clairvoyant powers, their use in diagnosis might be invaluable. This was a usable hypothesis for Dr Norman Shealy, a neurosurgeon and Director of the Rehabilitation Center in La Crosse, Wisconsin. Interest in the subject grew out of his awareness of his own psychic skills. To test the question, he designed an elaborate experiment which he describes in his presentation.

THE ROLE OF PSYCHICS IN MEDICAL DIAGNOSIS

Norman Shealy, M.D.

The first formal paper on the subject of psychic diagnosis was given in London in 1842 by John Elliotson. He was a physician and the first Professor of Medicine at University College, London. He was, I regret to say, ostracized by the medical community for his pains.

The problems of routine diagnosis are not as great as you might think. Traditional physicians are about eighty per cent accurate in their diagnosis of patients. Of course, once a patient has a case file or a lengthy history of treatment, diagnosis is even more accurate. None the less, I have examined clairvoyance as a diagnostic aid, in the hope that it will help to clear up some of our remaining problems, both of diagnosis and treatment.

Traditionally, over the past forty or fifty years, the doctor's approach has tended to be that of barber. We have been ready to destroy troublesome parts of the nervous system – 'If in doubt, cut it out.' Some of my colleagues have not been as bothered by this situation as they might have been. In my own opinion, lobotomies and the destruction of areas of the nervous system should play no part in the management of pain. A patient who loses part of his brain in the attempt to deal with suffering loses also part of his most precious possessions – his emotions, his power to react, and some of his freedom in the broad, spiritual sense. A person who has his spinal cord cut to control pain has only a 10 per cent chance of cure and a 130 per cent chance of complications. Yet thousands and thousands of these operations have been performed. Except in cancerous conditions, where there may perhaps be some justification for this kind of surgery, I have personally never undertaken it.

The alternative to surgery is drug medication. It is easy to see why this alternative appeals to doctors. Aside from questions of convenience and preferability to permanent surgery, doctors are continuously bombarded by advertising from drug companies. They assure us that the drugs they proffer are totally effective, harmless, free of side effects, non-addictive, non-toxic, and so on. Injectable toluene is described as non-narcotic, for example. Yet, in my opinion, it is one of the most addictive drugs on the market. Users suffer withdrawal seizures and often start taking it in even larger doses, so that their skin begins to look like dried orange peel.

The advertisements currently appearing in medical journals are indicative. On one page is the headline statement 'Think about Pain.' On the next page we read the words 'Now Think about Percadan.' Or again, you might see, 'You know all you have to do when faced with back pain is to give the patient a little Valium.' Actually, in my opinion, all that Valium does is to slow the patient's mind to the point where he stops complaining. It is in any case criminal that doctors are urged to think about treating pain before rendering a diagnosis. Similarly, with anxiety, you are urged simply to treat your patients with Librium or Librax or whatever. The advertisements are persuasive, pervasive and altogether insidious.

What is the statistical truth about drugs? We know for instance that placebos – harmless, chemically inert medications – are 50 per cent as effective as narcotics in dealing with pain. More important, and more damning still, one recent study of the total output of one of the major drug houses showed that only 25 per cent of their preparations produced the result that they are supposed to have. We were not told, unfortunately, what the drugs did instead – only that 25 per cent of them had the advertised effect.

I would go so far as to say that virtually all symptoms are psychosomatic. Something slightly in excess of 15 per cent of the patients a doctor sees have a physical, organic problem that has only psychosomatic overtones. That 15 per cent I will leave to the physicians. But there should be some alternative method to deal with the remaining 85 per cent.

An Alternative?

I chose to investigate the ability of a variety of clairvoyants to make a diagnosis, using a large number of patients. We required a base-line against which to measure or compare their ability, and the only base-line we could use was the opinions of doctors. But we tried to make the physician's estimate as objective and unbiased as possible.

Each of the patients involved in the study was given the Minnesota Multiphasic Personality Inventory. This is a standard test with a long history; we know a lot about it, its strengths and its limitations. It consists of 546 questions. The result is a graph that tells us, more or less, how sane or stable the patient is emotionally. The test is not perfect – no test is. On the whole, it can at best tell us whether or not someone is seriously disturbed. It is less helpful in milder cases.* The M.M.P.I. was used then as our main base-line and objective diagnostic aid on the personality side. But we did not stop there.

In our work we frequently administer other tests to the patients as well, particularly in those areas where the M.M.P.I. is not strong. Naturally we see and talk to the patients ourselves, and form an intuitive idea as to their mental clarity or confusion. One way and another, we end up with a fair idea as to whether the patient has any kind of

* This test, like most standardized tests, has built-in honesty and consistency measures. It is good on picking up hypochondria, depression and hysteria. It is less good on other personality traits and disorders – but · e do get some picture of the patient's sexual balance, tendency to manic-depression and so on.

mental or emotional conflict that is likely to aggravate his or her pain. All these additional diagnostic procedures were used to build up a profile of the patients who formed our study population in the experiment.

The next step is the physical inventory. We ask the patient where he or she is experiencing pain. We listen to what the patient tells us, come to a decision, and sketch this area or areas on a pictorial representation of the body. We also translate the information into anatomical terms. This is obviously one of the most objective items that we can use to test psychic diagnosis. Then we pin down the history of the pain. In our clinic we exclude individuals in whom the cause of pain is, in our opinion, purely emotional. All our patients have a physical basis to their illness. All of them, in fact, have had multiple surgery and have had drug treatments as well. Of course, because these patients have had so much surgery and medication, many have developed personality problems. They tend to manifest obvious psychosomatic conditions such as ulcers, troublesome bladders, menstrual cramps, and so on.

Intensity of pain was also included on the check-list. If a patient described his pain as severe, we accepted his evaluation and noted it. However, we also examined the patient's lifestyle to see how well he or she was coping. This produced a more factual estimate of how incapacitating the pain apparently was.

We were also generous to the psychics to the extent that we did not expect them to produce a full clinical description of the illness. It was sufficient if they said a patient had a physical problem with the eyes, the liver or what have you. Each psychic completed the check-list we prepared for each patient. This appears to be concrete – comparisons should prove easy. Unfortunately, the case is otherwise.

Clairvoyants are sensitives. In many ways they are like artists. Even if you have his voluntary co-operation, you cannot force an artist to produce. I personally am accustomed to working a twelve-hour day – even at times sixteen hours. Many individuals who are artistically inclined do not operate this way. You cannot get them, or expect them, to produce on a rigid time-schedule. It took us almost a year to persuade the psychics to generate just the first half of the charts we needed.

We chose a variety of psychic talents. We also wanted to know relatively how effective clairvoyance was in relation to palmistry, graphology and so on. In all we took three clairvoyants, one palmist, one graphologist, one numerologist and one astrologer.

The palmist received only a palm print, with the patient's name and the date when the print was taken. The graphologist had the most information – because the patient was required to write a one-page letter saying anything he wished. A patient may advertently or inadvertently have given some of his diagnosis in the letter. The clairvoyants did all their work from a photograph, with the patient's name and date of birth on the back in someone else's handwriting. The astrologer received only the name and birth date, and the numerologist the same.

Comparisons were to be made with the diagnoses I had arrived at by standard clinical procedures. But we also used further controls. First, we had a random test done by standard laboratory techniques, carried out by hand, not by computer. Second, we gave a professor of psychology, who claimed no clairvoyant abilities, a photograph and the name and date of birth of each patient. He looked at these and wrote down the first thing that came into his head.

The Results

The answers given by the psychics to the individual items on the questionnaire that they were required to complete ranged between twenty-five per cent accuracy (which is chance level) and eighty per cent (which represents a score three times above chance and is highly significant statistically).

The clairvoyants, who saw only a photograph of the patient with name and date of birth, proved to be the most accurate of all the psychics. The graphologist gave the least accurate diagnoses, while the psychologist, who claimed no psychic ability, proved that he had none – his scores did not exceed chance level and were at times below it.

The overall accuracy of the entire group of psychics was sixty per cent. That is more than twice as good as chance. But this is not as accurate as diagnosis generally. But it is equally true that we have a range and depth of access to these patients that was denied the psychics, plus all the most modern diagnostic tools. Moreover, we have not yet completed numerous cross-correlations among the replies of the individual psychics. It may be that if we consider only answers where three or more of the psychics agree, then their scoring level will rise still further. We have good reason to suspect that this will be the case, for in a semi-formal pilot study of seventeen or so patients that we ran with psychics, whenever there was a consensus of opinion among them they were ninety-eight per cent accurate on personality disorders. In the pilot study the psychics saw the patient for a few moments, but no words were exchanged. Those results are probably more accurate than the M.M.P.I. As to physical abnormalities in the pilot study, the psychics proved eighty per cent correct in their diagnoses when in agreement.

The results of the study so far show that, on the basis of extremely flimsy information, psychics can diagnose with an accuracy well in excess of chance.*

I believe the evidence obtained from this study is completely unequivocal. It is not as good as I had hoped for – but the results seem irrefutable proof of the claimed abilities of psychics. The question now is, what do I do with the evidence? How do I get the message across to the medical profession? Can I reach them? People often ask me, 'How does the A.M.A. feel about you, are you accepted?' I usually make some wry joke at that point, such as the one when the consultant says to his patient, 'When I said I wanted a second opinion, I didn't mean yours, Mrs Fairweather.'

The Treatment of Pain

Aside from diagnosis, there is the problem of treatment. This is both a very serious and difficult issue when you have a patient who has already had four or five operations, has been ill for the past twenty years, and by now hates doctors and

---

* I should also state here that I did not fill out any part of the control documents until after all the psychic answers were in. Hence there was no easy way that the information could have been acquired telepathically.

almost everyone else. Some may be ready for acupuncture, but others are not. Some may be willing to accept responsibility for their own illness, and some may not. Others prefer to treat themselves extensively before they come to you, and believe that they can cure themselves by diet or something still more exotic. Such patients often object vigorously if you try to force them into a therapeutic programme. They do not like having you point out to them that they have been sick for ten years. It is hard to get a patient to accept responsibility for his own health. Consequently, we have devised a comprehensive programme for managing patients with chronic pain. This includes a variety of techniques. The programme I present to our patients is a teaching programme. I am not treating them; I teach them how to live and how to control their own pain. I do this because I cannot do much about their pain. First, we wean them from drugs. Second, we forbid them to talk about pain. We tell them that if they talk about their pain we might discharge them. We tell them that we know they have pain and we accept its reality, but that it does no good to complain about it.

Next, the patients are treated with a variety of mechanical techniques. We find ice to be generally more effective than heat, but we use both. We also have a professional masseur. We also train staff to give patients very vigorous slapping massage in the areas that hurt. Some patients are hooked up to external electrical stimulators to vibrate the area where the pain is. These techniques actually help many. In about twenty-five per cent of cases they will totally control the pain. Those who are still around after a week or ten days of this kind of treatment start to receive acupuncture.

When the patients first arrive we begin to brainwash them. We use a combination of techniques under the general heading of autogenic training. This method was pioneered by a German psychiatrist, Johannes Schultz, in 1928. It is not hypnosis; it is mental self-suggestion. We find that if we can convince the patient that he can talk to his body and control his symptoms he will. While he is learning, he is also using biofeedback. We employ the standard techniques of biofeedback, including temperature control, brain wave control, muscle relaxation and, for general relaxation, the G.S.R. or galvanic skin response.

The biggest task we face is convincing the patient that he must take the responsibility for gaining control over the pain. For we have learned that the patient who, for instance, learns to put himself into an alpha state of brain activity – where the waves are steadily ticking away at around ten cycles per second – will not experience pain. It is impossible to perceive pain while in steady alpha state. By self-programming and practice, in two to ten months he will gain complete control over his pain.

The Use of Psychics in Medical Practice

I have yet to meet a psychic – and I have personally met some fifty or so – who was not a better psychologist than he was a clairvoyant. Their insight is often phenomenal. A couple had come to me. We had earlier treated the wife as a patient. When she came to us initially she was on a stretcher. When she left us she was 50 per cent improved in her physical activity, 500 per cent improved in her pain and 200 per cent improved in her mental attitude. From being a bed-ridden individual she had become almost self-sufficient. As a result, her husband no longer loved her. He did not like the idea of a relatively healthy mate. He said that if she could make this improvement now, she could have made it eight years ago. He was furious and resentful. He wanted to divorce her. I had no idea what to do with them. They had been to two marriage counsellors, one minister and three psychiatrists. Having survived all this treatment, the wife thought it was worth keeping her marriage intact.

Fortunately, on the day they came in one of the clairvoyants was with me. He is also a spiritualist minister. So I told the two of them about the 'visiting minister' we had on the premises. Why not go and pay him a visit? I took them in, expecting them to storm out twenty minutes later. But when I finally saw them after an hour and a half, the husband said to me, 'Doc, don't ever lose this man. He's the greatest thing you've got.'

It turned out that the psychic had given them insights that

I was quite incapable of giving them. He began by discussing with them the fact that their elder son was taking marijuana – which none of the rest of us knew, of course – and also talked about their other child and his problems. Then he started to discuss the husband's mistress – again none of us knew about this – and suggested to the husband he was only going to swap one clutch of problems for another. At this, apparently, the husband nearly collapsed – but he rallied, and the couple ended up a good deal closer.

Although I am satisfied that psychics can make good diagnoses, I am even more convinced that their best role is that of spiritual counsellor. But I think it is also appropriate that we should call on their help when we run into a diagnostic dilemma, as we do in about twenty per cent of cases. At that point we might use a team of three clairvoyants to give us leads, perhaps even a clear-cut diagnosis. This would not only improve the quality of medical service, but would perhaps help us to combat the excesses of surgery and drug medication which have made many of our patients even more sick than when they first encountered the medical care system.

CHAPTER IV

A New Medicine?

We believe in the medicine we have. This belief, even though blurring at the edges, sustains the medical enterprise. But the gap between what medicine can do and what the public assumes it can do is great. John Powles has this to say:

> Enthusiasm for the system has outpaced its concrete achievements and its indirect costs tend to be underplayed. Despite the evidence to the contrary, it is widely believed by both patients and their doctors that industrial populations owe their high health standards to "scientific medicine," that such medical technology as currently exists is largely effective in coping with the tasks it faces and that it offers great promise for the future.[1]

Powles is correct. But as evidence mounts about the relative inefficiency of medical care, and as it is slowly perceived that our health is not improving, the public may then recognize the limits of modern medicine and the need for new approaches. Nevertheless, another problem remains. Rashi Fein, a health economist at Harvard, argues that consumer demand is *the* most formidable obstacle to reform:

> In the case of health and medical care, we are dealing with a sector in which, because of customs and folkways, image may be even more important than reality. Because some (even relatively little) medical care deals with matters of life and death, because of fear, because of infatuation with science and technology – as well as because medicine oftentimes does help some individuals

and, therefore, each individual can hope that it will help him – persons have come to believe that medical care services and intervention by the physician make significant contributions to health. This view is not likely to change.[2]

It may be true that the public's perception of medical care will be difficult to change. But sometimes change can be very swift. George Leonard, in a perceptive article entitled 'How We Will Change',[3] postulates four elements which can be detected in the dynamics of change: new perceptions; positive vision, myth, 'story'; a new theory; and a specific model or example of the change.

In the case of medical care, which Leonard uses in an example, many of the 'perceptions' of the investigators that are reflected in this volume meet the first criterion. And as the limits of modern medicine are recognized, the concomitant is the 'version' of the new holistic medicine – the second criterion. Then, many of the ideas discussed in the presentations offered at the May Lectures, if linked together to create a cogent framework, will contribute towards a general theory of health – the third criterion. Such a theory is far from worked out, but many of the elements have been identified. Once this process is completed, and it should be in a few more years, all that will be missing will be specific models – the fourth criterion – which incorporate the emerging theory, although there may in fact be some 'models' already in operation. There is nothing rigidly sequential about the four steps. Carl Simonton's practice may be a model. Elmer Green's laboratory work with biofeedback another, and Norman Shealy's 'pain' clinic still another.

A new medicine cannot be clearly seen. And its evolution is not certain. It may also be very slow in evolving, or may simply be the consequence of a series of incremental modifications of today's medicine. But, on balance, it seems that a new medicine will emerge. The purpose of this book has been to accelerate that process.

Three Essays on the Changes We Are Facing

David Tansley's presentation opens doors that have been opened before, and promptly shut. The 'rationalistic' bias of Western culture is uncongenial to this sort of thinking. Yet even to the Western mind, there is a way of 'fitting' in what Tansley has to say. Much of what he schematizes is incomprehensible to many, not because of the terminology but because it explores information which, to those who grasp it, can only be experienced. A transcendental experience leaves the subject with an intuitive, essentially non-verbal experience. The charts and diagrams are efforts to reduce the experience to the verbal representation level. It is hard to do. But one thing is nevertheless clear: for some, mystical experience yields insights about health and well-being, which, however esoterically communicated, are not necessarily false. To put it another way, they are neither true nor false because they are experiential.

A NEW ANATOMY FOR A NEW MEDICINE

David V. Tansley, D.C.

Andreas Vesalius, the eminent sixteenth-century anatomist and physician, firmly maintained that the study of the human soul was within the province of anatomy. Clearly there are different approaches to gaining an understanding of the nature of man. On the one hand the physician sees man through the eyes of science. He is concerned with that which is objective and tangible, with what can be observed by physical means, and as a result he has basically a mechanistic view of man. On the other hand, a sixteenth-century physician such as Vesalius reflects a broader approach, because he not only concerned himself with the physical aspects of man but with the more intangible and spiritual factors as well. His sensitivity, his inner awareness, enabled him to state that the study of the soul of man lay within the province of anatomy. With men of his stature such statements arise from a direct perception; they are not made lightly, and above all else they hold hints for those who are capable of discerning them – hints which can lead the inquirer into whole new areas of knowledge, provided of course he feels he still has something to learn about the nature of man.

If we accept the existence of the soul we can formulate a new anatomy – new, that is, from the orthodox point of view. To me a new anatomy means a concept of total man in terms of a series of interpenetrating, interacting energy systems in which the physical form is seen simply as an externalization, as a reflection, as a product of their activity which is utilized as a vehicle of experience by the soul. This concept embraces the hypothesis that man is triune in nature, that he is spirit, soul and body – or if you prefer life, consciousness and form. In other words, I mean an anatomy of man that is concerned with the reality behind the outward appearance; an anatomy that deals with causative factors and not just effects; one that recognizes that the terms spirit and soul are simply names given to energic systems which, although they are invisible, do in fact have structure and form . . . and that the qualities and activities arising in these systems give birth and direction to the personality of man in his life on the physical, emotional and mental levels of his being.

This new anatomy draws its contents from all that is found to be useful and practical in the ancient teachings of India, China, Tibet, Egypt and Greece, and from the writings of the medieval medical philosophers of Europe. Such knowledge, if synthesized with our modern scientific data, would provide an anatomy of total man which would not only revolutionize the doctor's view of the patient but, and this is equally important, the patient's view of himself.

He would no longer be, as is often the case, a medical statistic shorn of his dignity, fragmented into a 'heart case' or a 'lung case', and reduced to a number on the folder of his case history. He would be a total being with a place and a role to work out in the universal field of life wherein he lives, an individual with a destiny and purpose that can be seen to be inextricably linked with all life. In short, values which enable man to conduct his life properly and reach correct moral and aesthetic judgments would be restored within the framework of science which, despite its great contributions to humanity, neither deals in values nor helps man to understand his life nor gives meaning to it. The concern of science is of course with that which can be observed, measured and weighed, but in spite of itself it is tripping headlong into areas of knowledge which lie beyond in the subtler realms of nature. It is rapidly exhausting the mechanistic, material concept of life, and it is in fact already discovering certain aspects of the subtle anatomy of man.

These discoveries will give rise to a new medicine. By a new medicine I mean a healing art which recognizes the true nature of man and his place within the scheme of things, a healing art that is both philosophic and scientific in its approach to the problems of health and disease. I mean a healing art in which all disciplines – be they medical, chiropractic, osteopathic or naturopathic – function as a co-operative whole, devoid of political exclusiveness or imagined superiority and motivated only by service to the patient as an individual and humanity as a whole. The suffering that people undergo because of separative attitudes arising out of archaic orthodox codes of conduct has to be seen to be believed.

The new medicine would to a great extent place back into the hands of the patient responsibility for understanding and taking care of his own health. It would play a far greater educative role in the philosophic sense and, on a co-operative basis with both the patient and other disciplines, it would seek to identify those factors in a man's life which give rise to inharmony and ultimately disease. They could then together take constructive, logical steps to eradicate these factors rather than automatically issue a drug prescription as is the practice today. Laurens van der Post, in the T.V. series on the work of Carl Jung, said that it was so sad to see the tensions and anxieties of patients, which in reality expressed their inner spiritual awakening, suppressed through the indiscriminate use of prescribed drugs. Of course this calls for practitioners with a depth of knowledge and understanding that is rare, but hopefully today such individuals are on the increase; they combine within themselves an open mind, sound professional knowledge and some understanding of the real nature of man. From such people and their work a new medicine will arise, one that is concerned with the real causes of disease rather than the suppression of effects through chemotherapy.

Tansley is driving at what is generally referred to as 'intuitive knowledge', which he distinguishes from other forms of knowledge in the following way.

It is possible to divide knowledge broadly into three categories. First, there is theoretical knowledge. This is basically the knowledge accepted by the average untrained mind and utilized for the purposes of everyday living. Secondly, there is discriminate knowledge which is derived essentially from the scientific approach: it analyzes and determines those factors which in a given area can be measured and proved. It enables man to arrive at truths relative to the world he lives in, to eliminate non-essentials and to arrive at a body of knowledge that can be verified by other trained minds. This kind of knowledge gives man the power to enter areas of life which remain locked and mysterious to the untrained mind.

There is, however, a third body of knowledge – the intuitive. Intuitive knowledge is that which is known by the soul and which emerges through the mind into the brain of the individual. I would like you to note the sequence of soul, mind and brain, for these three have to reach a point of mutual resonance for intuitive knowledge to register in the consciousness of man. What I am in effect saying is that there lies beyond our accepted scientific body of knowledge a far greater dimension of knowledge, a knowledge that is both scientific and esoteric, filled with spiritual values. It is an area of knowledge from which the inner spiritual man can wield great power; it is an area from which he has dominion over Nature. It is a realm of knowledge which we in this period of transition need, in order to balance the excesses of the mechanistic approach to life which give rise to much of the tension that people experience today, and which have contributed very largely to the pollution of earth and man over the last few decades.

There are many people who can actually see the subtle anatomy of man and observe its interaction with the physical organic systems. Some interesting data can be found on this in Dr Karagula's book, *Breakthrough to Creativity.*[1] She has worked with sensitives who can see and describe the nature of the subtle anatomy, and who can also outline areas in the energy bodies where physical pathological states arise – often before they become organic lesions.

The idea that man's physical body is simply the externalization of other invisible, subtle forms which embody life is very old. One finds evidence of this in virtually every civilization throughout the world, and it is a concept that has survived for thousands of years. The very persistence of this idea should persuade us that it is worth exploring.

Today, of course, it is fashionable to dismiss such a concept as superstitious nonsense from a pre-scientific age and to throw out the idea. This is remarkable when one stops to think that science and medicine as we know them today grew from the work and knowledge gathered and applied by some very clever men in the past; men like Galen, Hippocrates, Paracelsus, Vesalius and many others, who saw no great distinction between the spiritual and physical aspects of their species. Paracelsus, no mean critic of the medicine of his day, said, 'Nature has within itself forces visible and invisible, bodies visible and invisible, and all are natural.' More true to form, he also said, 'The mere looking at externals is a matter for clowns, but the intuiting of internals is a secret which belongs to physicians.'

So let us look at some of these 'internals' of which Paracelsus spoke. Figure 5 below shows that man in his totality is a trinity. He is spirit, soul and body – or life, consciousness and form. The form we know something about. This can be represented by a square divided into four sections. The lowest is the dense body we can see, next comes the electrodynamic aspect of man, above that is the emotional nature and at the top is the mental aspect. This quaternary forms the personality of man. Above the personality, or lower-self, is the soul represented by a circle. As far as the ancients were concerned, the soul was an aspect of the mental apparatus of man, so they divided the mind into two distinct parts – namely, the abstract mind containing the soul and the concrete or intellectual mind which we recognize as part of the personality.

Beyond the soul lies the spirit of man, the real inner spiritual being. This is represented by a triangle symbolizing the one containing the three.

If we take these three symbols and use them to draw an analogy with the nervous system of man, we will have an interesting insight into the nature of the relationship between spirit, soul and form as well as into the problem and difficulty of coming to grips with an understanding of subtle

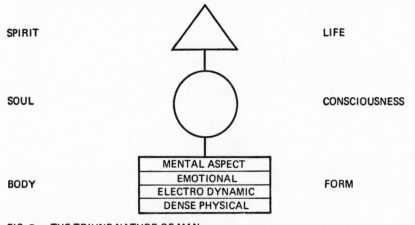

FIG. 5   THE TRIUNE NATURE OF MAN

anatomy. The unit of the nervous system is called a neuron, and each neuron ends in a bundle of fibres known as dendrites. The area across which nerve impulses are conveyed from one neuron to another is called a synapse.

By drawing in the nerve fibres to join spirit, soul and body, we have a very accurate analogy of what actually happens in the relationship between the various bodies of man (see Figure 6, below). It is important to note that there is no physical contact between the nerve fibres at the synapse and, just as there is a gap between the down-reaching neuron from the spiritual triad and the up-reaching neuron of the form aspect, so there is such a gap or synaptic cleft in the actual physical nervous system.

In our bodies, for a nerve impulse to bridge that gap, a chemical reaction has to occur; so it is with total man, if the gap is to be bridged between the concrete, lower intellectual mind and the levels of the abstract mind and the soul. But here the reaction is not so much chemical as alchemical. Man has to learn to bridge that gap, to cross that cosmic diaphragm, eventually to build a link consciously. When he does, then he has access to a whole vast new world; he lets go of the 'power trip' of the lower mind and has what we call an open mind. Until then, there tends to be a rigid attitude of looking at things – one that shuts out any comprehension,

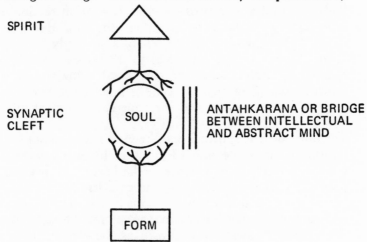

FIG. 6   NEURON ANALOGY IN THE SUBTLE ANATOMY OF MAN

for example, of the subtle bodies of man, and much else besides.

Now let us deal with the esoteric constitution of man, from the top downwards, since this is the logical sequence (see Figure 7, opposite). The spirit of man is said to be a spark of the universal mind, an outbursting of the universal mind, and as such to be triune in nature. This spark is referred to as the monad, and is the true spiritual, immortal man which incarnates time and again. The monad has been defined as a system of energy which under specific circumstances will produce a specific form and/or sequence of events. Apart from the energy aspect, it has two other aspects – awareness or subjectivity and its objective existence. In Christian terminology the first aspect is called the Father, the second the Son and the third the Holy Spirit. They may also be called the energies of will, love-wisdom and active intelligence. Alternatively, we may think of them in terms of positive energy, balanced energy and negative energy.

On a larger scale in our solar system we can see these three aspects working out in the following manner. The will aspect is the basis of systematic movement, of driving forward through space. The love aspect is the basis of cyclic spiral movement and the law of attraction and repulsion. This law is clearly seen in action when one considers the cells of our body; they are governed by the law of attraction and repulsion, a breakdown in either direction resulting in disease. The law of attraction enables our body to keep its form; the law of repulsion sees to it that each life or cell retains its individuality. If this breaks down, tumorous growths make their appearance. The intelligence aspect is the basis of rotary motion and the spheroidal form of all that exists.

The inner or true spiritual man, then, is triune in nature and manifests upon the monadic plane. In order to become conscious and gain experience in the lower and increasingly coarser levels of matter, the monad casts its 'shadow' into the 'far country' or physical plane. This it does through a series of force centres known as permanent atoms. There are five of them plus another centre known as the mental unit, and each of these forms a stable force centre around which the

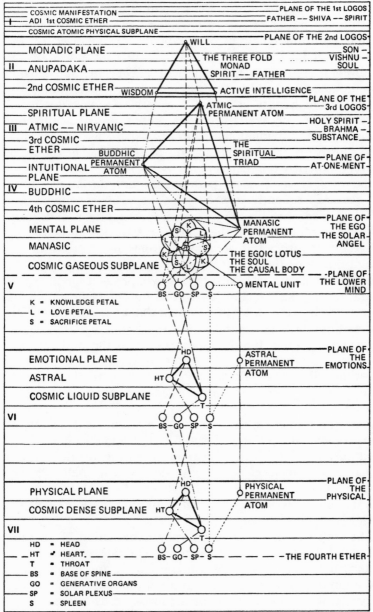

Taken from *Treatise on Cosmic Fire* by Alice Bailey (Lucis Trust)

FIG. 7 THE ESOTERIC CONSTITUTION OF MAN

subtle bodies are built. Permanent atoms are under the attractive power of the love-wisdom aspect of the monad, and the ordinary atoms of our bodies are vitalized by the mother or intelligence aspect. The permanent atoms are the storehouses of past life experience. They are the karmic computers if you like, and through them is determined the nature and quality of each life experience; what quality of vehicles will be available, what proportions of health and disease the individual can expect to experience – depending, of course, on how he conducts his present life. The nature of every experience is determined by what has been stored in the memory banks of the permanent atoms during past lives. They are frequently referred to as the 'arbiters of fate'.

The monad, then, in the process of incarnating, sounds forth its note; it breathes out the word, the A.U.M. This drives the lives constituting the permanent atoms into a state of activity; they become magnetic and draw to themselves various grades of matter to form vehicles of expression for the spiritual man. Like the God he lives within, he begins to create and to breathe life and consciousness into form. This breathing forth causes the will aspect to link with the Atmic permanent atom, the wisdom aspect with the Buddhic permanent atom and the intelligence aspect with the Manasic permanent atom. Thus the inner man reflects himself outwards through a triangle of energies called the spiritual triad.

Now the monad must create a semi-permanent vehicle of expression on the higher aspect of the mental plane as an outpost of consciousness. It cannot penetrate any deeper into matter and must set up a body which can mediate between itself and the coarser levels of matter and the physical plane. This vehicle is the central office for information exchange and is called the soul.

The soul comes into being through the action of energies flowing through the spiritual triad. The positive energies of spirit meet the negative energies of matter and give birth to the son or soul in man. The nature of the soul is light and in form it is a lotus of twelve petals surrounding a latent point of fire, frequently referred to as the jewel in the heart of the lotus (see Figure 8, opposite).

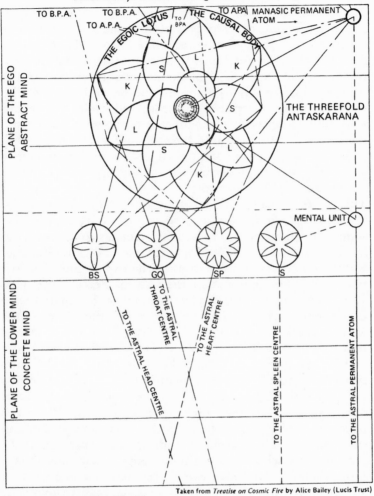

Taken from *Treatise on Cosmic Fire* by Alice Bailey (Lucis Trust)

A.P.A. = ATMIC PERMANENT ATOM
B.P.A. = BUDDHIC PERMANENT ATOM

K = KNOWLEDGE PETAL
L = LOVE PETAL
S = SACRIFICE PETAL

BS = BASE OF SPINE
GO = GENERATIVE ORGANS
SP = SOLAR PLEXUS
S = SPLEEN

FIG. 8   THE COSMIC GASEOUS SUBPLANE

The lotus of the soul, just like the vehicles of the lower-self, has to evolve and develop: it is no more perfect as a vehicle of expression than the lower-self in its early stages of development. The unfolding of the soul comes about through the impact of experiences of the personality of man in the three worlds; this is feedback in the deepest sense of the word. As man develops his knowledge and ability to love and serve and sacrifice his own interests for those of the group, these qualities are built into the soul, and from a rather dull and relatively lifeless condition it begins to radiate colour and activity until it becomes a radiant sphere of light in which each petal is opened to the full.

The twelve petals have some rather interesting analogies. For example, they have been related to the twelve signs of the zodiac which cover the sum total of man's experience and must of course be built into the soul. In the Book of Revelations there are references to the twelve gates and the twelve foundation stones to the City of Peace, Jerusalem. Jesus told his disciples, twelve in number, to repair to the upper chamber for the Last Supper; and in the picture of the soul we have the twelve petals of disciples grouped around that central point of energy which is the Christ at the centre of the chamber of the soul, the three inner petals being symbolic of those disciples present at his transfiguration. On the physical plane, these twelve petals of the solar lotus manifest or externalize themselves as the twelve cranial nerves. One of them, the vagus nerve, is seen to link the head (representing spirit in man) to the heart (representing the soul) and on below to the viscera (which is analogous to the form of man). This nerve is often referred to as the path for the breath of the Holy Spirit, and is the road traversed by Joseph and Mary between Bethlehem and Jerusalem.

The soul, then, is the vehicle of manifestation for the spirit. Now in order to enter more deeply into matter, the soul itself must create a means by which it can gain experience. For this purpose it appropriates material from the mental, astral and etheric levels, sounds its own note and drives the personality into manifestation. Just as the spiritual triad is produced by the monad and gives rise to the soul, so the soul itself produces a triple form consisting of a mental body, an emotional body and an etheric body – and out of these arises the fourth and physical form.

The mental body, which consists of matter drawn from the mental levels, forms the concrete mind – the thinking, intellectual apparatus of the inner man. Used properly, it acts as a discriminative tool which helps the soul to determine the real from the unreal. Overdeveloped along strictly intellectual lines, it can reach such a state of power that it shuts off any impulses flowing from the soul into the personality. Then the mind, as the ancient texts put it, becomes the slayer of the real.

The emotional body, sometimes called the desire or astral body, is the form in which the interplay of emotions are felt – in which the person experiences the pairs of opposites such as pleasure and pain, happiness and depression. It is the body in which most people are polarized and certainly it is the one activated by drugs, particularly those that are hallucinogenic in nature.

A bad acid trip leads the individual to experience the lower levels of the astral plane, where he may see all manner of evil-looking forms and demons or plumb the depths of fear. On the other hand, he may find his way into the higher levels where all appears to be beautiful and filled with colour. Here, what seem to be mystical experiences or profound expressions of cosmic awareness occur. No matter if the trip is good or bad, it is an astral phenomenon and illusory in nature. Often the use of such drugs strips away insulation which Nature has used to seal off certain areas of awareness, which belong to a time that lies far back in pre-history. When this happens the soul of the person involved fails to achieve its goal for that particular life, and much energy is wasted sealing off these areas again. The aim of man today should be to use and develop his mental body, to bring his emotional body into a state of quietness and to align them with the soul and the Buddhic vehicle wherein the Christ principle is located.

Between the dense physical body and the emotional body is the body of vitality which is called the etheric body. The etheric body has been described as a network of energy lines permeated with fire, or as a web animated by a golden light.

The Bible speaks of it as the 'golden bowl'. It can best be described as a field of energy which underlies every atom and cell of the physical body, permeating every part of it and extending beyond to form a part of what is called the health aura. The etheric body then is the matrix, the archetype, upon which the physical form is erected.

This etheric framework consists of material drawn from the four ethers, creating a network of fine tubular channels which are related to the cerebro-spinal and sympathetic nervous systems. The integral unit formed by the etheric and physical bodies of man is vitally important, as the etheric body connects the physical world with the subtle inner worlds; through it the five senses are able to function on the physical plane, and progressively it is able to register and transmit the energies flowing to it from the soul.

The etheric body can be equated with the electrodynamic field of man, which can be measured with a vacuum tube volt meter. If one makes a thorough study of the etheric body in the various writings of the past, and then relates them directly to the work of Dr Saxton Burr as outlined in his book *Blueprint for Immortality*,[2] there is more than a passing similarity. Here one can find direct correlation of the ancient and modern knowledge concerning this vital form. Discovery of the etheric body by science will constitute one of the major breakthroughs in medicine during this century, and it is a breakthrough that has in fact already begun.

If you have read the books of Carlos Castaneda, you will recognize that don Juan is speaking of the etheric body when he tells Castaneda that men look like eggs filled with thousands of fibres of light, bristling and luminous, bursting in all directions. He further points out that everything is in touch with everything else through these light fibres, and that a man is a luminous egg of energy fibres, be he a beggar or a king. This is very reminiscent of the Aka threads that Max Freedom Long describes in his writings on the Polynesian Kahunas; these threads connect every life-form. The etheric body of the planet is of course something all life shares in common and it is the basis of brotherhood, as yet unrecognized. Like the soul it is a mediator; like the soul it is in the process of revelation.

Within each of the bodies of the personality are centres of force known as chakras. Carl Jung referred to them as the gateways of consciousness. They are like vortices of energy – five lie along the spine, one on the forehead and one on the vertex or crown of the head. Through them pass a variety of energies, which galvanize man into activity and determine the quality of his physical body, his character traits, his emotional attitude and his response to his inner and outer environment. Each chakra externalizes as an endocrine gland and governs certain areas of the physical form. It is interesting to note that the ancients listed both the pineal and thymus glands as endocrine. This is something which modern medicine has just discovered.

Ninety-five per cent of all disease is said to originate in the etheric and emotional bodies of man. Much of it is due to the improper functioning of the chakras. If this is so, then there is a whole new area for research into the nature and origin of disease as energy imbalance rather than gross organic pathology.

The soul finally clothes itself in dense physical matter, and the body we are so familiar with comes into being. This is a form rich in symbolism and often spoken of as the temple of the living God. Like a temple it has three divisions; the first two are the abdominal area, or outer court, and the third is the thorax, or inner court, which contains the heart and lungs. These two courts are divided by the diaphragm, symbol of the etheric body. Both are surmounted by the head, the holy of holies, repository of the spiritual will of the inner man. The entire human form, if studied in the light of the ancient wisdom, is filled with meaning for all who can read its message.

This, then, is a very brief and simplified outline of the subtle anatomy – the anatomy of total man. If one studies the subject with an open mind, accepting as a working hypothesis that man has a soul, then the way will open to simplicity in both the theory and practice of the healing art. Simplicity is a factor desperately needed in these days of overspecialization. The journey, as I have said, needs an open mind. The reward is access to a whole new dimension which can enrich the healing arts and, in fact, all departments of life. The Delphic injunction, 'Man, know thyself,' is as relevant today as when it was uttered.

If David Tansley's arguments are hard to swallow, what follows will undoubtedly cause many to gag. It is not easy to explain much of what Uri Geller can apparently do; much less to comprehend the rationale that Puharich offers. Indeed one sympathetic observer, Andrew Weil, author of *The Natural Mind,* remains befuddled. In his articles on Geller which recently appeared in *Psychology Today,*[3] Weil started a doubter, became a believer, returned to doubt, and then concluded that the whole thing is probably in the mind of the beholder.

IN DEPTH STUDIES OF URI GELLER
Andrija Puharich, M.D.

There has been enormous controversy in England recently about Uri Geller, most of it in the form of opposition. As a result, a good deal of distortion has arisen in the reports about his work. My aim is to set the record straight and report the story as it actually unfolded.

Perhaps I can best illustrate the perceptions people have about Uri's work and abilities with a story. This story concerns a man, Joe, who had a new gun dog that he was anxious to test. He took him out into the marshes and eventually some ducks flew over. The man shot one. The dog, without any instructions, walked over the water, retrieved the bird and brought it back to the man sitting in the blind. This was too much for the poor gentleman, so he abandoned his shooting and went back to the farm. Having thought the matter over seriously, he decided to invite his neighbour, Bill, on a shoot the next day to see if he would see the same thing. They arrived at the blind and soon some ducks flew overhead. The men shot, two ducks fell, and the dog took off

over the water to retrieve the birds. At this, Joe turned to Bill and asked, 'Did you see what I just saw?' 'Yep,' said Bill. 'Well, what do you think?' insisted Joe. 'Well,' said Bill, 'I don't believe that dog can swim.'
We face the same problem with Uri Geller.

Some Experiments at S.R.I.

Let me tell you about a few of the things Geller has done under strictly controlled conditions. The experiments I refer to were conducted by scientists at the Stanford Research Institute. Some of the accounts are due to appear in scientific journals.* There is, however, about a year's lag between an experiment and its appearance in the journals. In Uri Geller's case, unfortunately, there are perhaps also other reasons why the scientists are dragging their feet about publication.
I am sure you know that some magicians claim to be able to do, and in some cases can actually do, feats similar to Geller. But the tests that Uri has undergone at Stanford were very stringent. In tests where drawings and other events are duplicated, for example, he was locked up in what they call a shielded room. No signals of any kind can penetrate,

---

* In a paper published in *Nature*, vol. 251 (London, October 18th, 1974), page 602, the Stanford Research Institute reports on three tests with Uri Geller. Two of these they considered successful – one involved telepathy and the other clairvoyance.
There has been considerable controversy over the report in *Nature*, over leading articles by Dr Joseph Hanlon of the *New Scientist* on the S.R.I. report and on other Geller tests with groups of scientists in London.
In view of the controversy, perhaps one of the most interesting reactions from establishment science comes from Professor Halsted of Birkbeck College, who refers to his work with Geller in the *New Scientist* of October 17th, 1974:

> We have recently submitted a paper to *Nature* containing a more detailed still-all-too-brief report of four sessions and concluding as follows ... We feel that if similar sessions continue to be held, instances of this kind might accumulate, so that there will be no room for reasonable doubt that some new process is involved here, which cannot be accounted for or explained in terms of the laws of Physics at present known. Indeed we feel that we have very nearly reached that point ...

assuming that Uri had a confederate on the outside. The 'target' for Uri may consist of random numbers spewed out by a computer, or designs drawn by a computer on a randomly programmed basis. No one knows what these numbers or designs will be until they are actually turned out by the computer. At the point where Uri reproduces them they are, if anything, only potentials adrift in the memory bank of the computer – a set of electrical potentials among which a random selection will be made. Under these conditions Uri has produced a regular one to one correspondence between his own recorded attempts and the material subsequently produced by the computer.

The important point here is that the tests and scientific controls are stringent; they are 'cheat-proof'. No deception or trickery was possible under the conditions at S.R.I. Scientists are therefore faced with the problem that there is no existing scientific explanation for what Geller has done and can do.

Another experiment involved clairvoyance or precognition. A die is shaken in a steel box. Uri has to guess the face which the die will show in advance. He writes his guess on a piece of paper and hands it to the experimenters. Then and only then is the box shaken and the die ejected. Uri again was one hundred per cent accurate in this test. There is no conventional explanation. A great many scientists are currently seeking to understand these baffling results.

A further test to which Uri has been subjected is as follows. A one-gramme mass is placed on an electronic balance under a bell jar. There is no direct, 'normal' way of affecting the balance under these conditions. Uri, however, can concentrate on this mass and make it heavier or lighter. The results are read out on automatic strip charts so no human error is involved. These experimental results again contain the most shattering implications for the theoretical basis of physics.

Uri can also produce changes in magnetic fields, as registered by gauss meters – devices which measure increases or decreases in magnetic fields. No explanation currently exists for this phenomenon.

Yet a further example is Uri's ability to interfere with tape and video systems. By concentrating on the television screen Uri is able to affect the display, to make scenes and people dissolve and disappear. Examination of the equipment shows that Uri is able to erase the signals from the tapes.

A rather different ability Uri has demonstrated involves living systems. He has experimentally demonstrated his ability to cause an unopened flower bud to open. He takes the closed bud in his shut hand, concentrates on it briefly, and in a matter of seconds his hand is forced open. In his hand is a full blossom. I once saw him do this in the lobby of the Royal Garden Hotel. On a display cart were some very tiny radishes, less than a centimetre in diameter – looking more like peas. I asked Uri if he thought he could mature one of them quickly. He said he would try. In about ten seconds he held a radish the size of a tomato.

Another form of this control over living systems is the reverse of this process. In this demonstration bean sprouts three or four days into growth and several inches tall are used. Again, Uri holds them in his hand, concentrates on them, opens his hand, and there in the palm is the original bean. The sprout and all disappear. If this bean is replanted, it will grow again normally. The organic structure of the plant is in no way damaged.

Still another demonstration is frightening to some. Uri can cause living creatures to disappear and reappear somewhere else. I first began these experiments with him three years ago in Israel. We used frogs – normal, complete frogs. Uri was capable of making them disappear and reappear at other points. I should add that we never lost a frog. We progressed to mice and rats and then to pet animals. The latter interested us because we wanted to know whether any significant change occurred in the animal's personality or psychology as a result of the process. Occasionally these events happened unpremeditatedly. My pet dog disappeared before the eyes of a number of witnesses and reappeared outside the grounds of my residence.

Apart from living creatures, Uri can demonstrate the same process with complex physical mechanisms. The following experiment was also conducted at the Stanford Research Institute laboratory. The team was headed by Captain Edgar Mitchell. A watch was sealed in an iron box on which one of the experimenters sat. Uri's task was to cause the object to disappear from within the box and to land upon a test platform consisting of a flat loose-sided table, which was observed from underneath by a camera, from two sides by other cameras and from above by a video-camera. After two hours, all the experimenters clearly saw a watch fall from the ceiling and land on the test platform. Oddly enough, at that instant three of the cameras were simultaneously disabled. A part of one dematerialized, another malfunctioned, and the third sustained a power failure. Fortunately, the video-camera continued to function and recorded the event. The watch, upon examination, was undamaged, and it bore the correct serial number. It was also found to be missing from the iron box. How is one to interpret these events? Can we explain them by the use of natural laws? Or are we dealing with something like the dog in my story, which walked on water?

The Explanation

I began a series of rather intensive studies with Uri in Israel in December 1971. My own hypothesis was that some kind of intelligent energy must lie behind these phenomena; they could not be the result of uncontrolled or blind forces. The only way I could think of approaching the question was to hypnotize Uri in order to explore his experiences, both conscious and unconscious, which might contain clues as to how the apparently intelligent energy was manifested.

At first we produced a fairly standard mediumistic phenomenon – a voice spoke through Geller which claimed to be the voice of another being. Calling itself Spectra, the voice said it was from a distant part of the universe. It described itself as an intelligent being, though not of a type that we could readily recognize. It was the source of these phenomena around Geller. I was not especially happy about this information because it was 'filtered' through a human being, with all the distortions and theoretrical problems that were implicit in the process. Fortunately, we discovered a method whereby we could externalize the phenomenon. We found that if an ordinary cassette tape-recorder was placed on the table between Uri and myself, often the 'start' button would be pressed down by some paranormal agency and then a tape-recorded message would be broadcast. The imprintation was apparently placed directly on the tape. The signal that a communication was about to start was usually some paranormal happening, like a pitcher floating up off the table.

The voice on the tape-recorder was synthetic. Such voices can readily be manufactured or put together using electronic signals. The messages or communications were very clear and very concise. I have recorded many of these. They are excerpted in my recent book about Uri. What impressed me far more than the communications themselves or the fact that it was possible to converse with the voice – although, of course, the matter of imprinting of voice direct on to tape is itself remarkable – was the fact that the tape would dematerialize after the sessions. Usually I was given time to transcribe the communication verbatim, but when I had done that, the tape vanished. I have watched it do so in front of my eyes.

I could not possibly relate all the contents of some sixty-seven communications. In brief summary only, therefore, the gist of the communications is this. There are beings who have been observing man for some thousands of years. They exist not simply on another planet but outside our space-time network. They have mastered what we would call time-travel, although this is an inadequate concept. They claim to have a connection with what are popularly known as flying saucers. They say that this shape is the representation of themselves and their mode of travel, that happens to arise when they switch to our space-time dimension.[4]

Naturally, I have quizzed these alleged communicants about their reasons for being here and for having chosen Uri as their prime channel. They do not give clear-cut answers to these questions, but their replies can be summed up something like this: Uri has the necessary biological make-up to handle this kind of energy without harm to himself. This is really the sole reason for the choice. There is no reason of his having Messiah-like attributes or abilities. There is a question, however, of his having a sufficiently equable and likeable personality to be able to work with – in the sense of perform before – many different kinds of people. He is a good representative.

The voices, or beings, further suggest that they appear regularly at intervals of three thousand years or so to, as it were, 'take our temperature' – to see whether we are ready for more open communication. A figure like Uri is a 'test case'. He and the feats he performs are attention-getters. People see him, watch him, think about him, relate to him. Their reactions are studied and these are the data which the alleged beings are seeking.

Now of course, I can only put this to you. In a sense I think of myself, like Uri, as a witness, in the religious sense of that term. That is, I feel it incumbent on me to talk about what I have seen and heard, and about its possible significance for mankind. I should perhaps add here that we have had, particularly from Scandinavia, reports of sick individuals being cured through watching Uri on television. It would be and is quite wrong to think of Uri and what he does as mere isolated 'stunts'. The effect Uri is having on the world in general is both a great and a diverse one. His hope and my hope is that people are being introduced through him to another level of consciousness, another level of being.

Werner Erhard is the founder and major force behind E.S.T., Erhard Seminars Training. E.S.T. is a short-term course in reality – a blend of Esalen philosophy with Western verbal pyrotechnics. Erhard's presentation, like Vogel's, had to be experienced to be believed – and perhaps understood. So much of his message depends on how he says what he says and how the listener experiences what he says – and less on what he says in fact. Yet the essay in written form has a driving kind of energy – a sort of pell-mell 'logic'. But to make any sense, it must be read quickly, without undue cognitive masturbation. It also helps if you hold your breath.

CONSCIOUSNESS AND COMMITMENT

Werner Erhard

I do not want to talk to you about the E.S.T. training. I do not want to talk to you about E.S.T. because I cannot talk to you about it in an hour. There is nothing that I could tell you that would be meaningful, except that people after they do it seem to experience life in some dimensions which they had not especially experienced before and their experience of satisfaction in particular seems to expand. Beyond that I could give you a whole bunch of explanations which I have dreamt up to try to explain experience, but all I would be doing is just that – giving you a whole bunch of explanations to try to explain.

The first thing I tell people if I am going to do a training with them is that they are not experiencing. That always bothers people because they know very well that they are experiencing. If someone is experiencing some discomfort in life and I say, 'Well, if you would experience it would go away,' they get very annoyed, because the discomfort is very real for them.

One of the things I would like to be clear about is that E.S.T. training is built upon the idea that there is something different between experience and reality: that what is real is not necessarily experiential. It takes, in the normal course of events, about eight hours to do this, and we have only an hour or so to do it. I shall, therefore, be glossing over some of the points. In addition, I would normally need your active co-operation in the way in which I do it. In the six- or eight-hour version I try to put out what I call 'fish hooks' in order to catch on to people's 'yes, buts'. For instance, if I say up is down, you say 'Yes, but it does not look that way to me' – then I can deal with your 'yes, but'. You then tell me how it feels to you and I can acknowledge that that is the way it feels to you. You can go on to tell me about an experience you once had which relates to what we are talking about and so on. You then get a chance to express whatever comes up in you, and I say whatever I say. For instance, Carl and Stephanie Simonton's talk pointed out that cancer is such a highly charged subject that many people are not able to feel anything about it; they just run away from it. And if you do get them to talk about it, then it proves to have a big emotional charge. If I said that blue is a colour, there would be a response in you. In other words, some things evoke in you a memory perhaps, a sensation in your body an attitude, who knows what. Well, I am going to ask you to do something very strange tonight. What I would like you to do is to *disbelieve* anything I say. Now that is a very difficult thing to do because we usually operate on a level of certainty one way or the other, in which we either believe something or we do not believe it. In other words, we feel we have to take a position with respect to it. Either it fits into the set of agreements that we have, or it is antagonistic to the set of agreements that we have. As a rule, if it does not fit in, if it is antagonistic, then we feel a need to reject it in order to protect our existing set of agreements. If it does fit in, we feel the need to accept it or, more accurately, to grab on to it because it reinforces our set of agreements.

Again, I would like you to be very clear about what I want you to do with the information I am going to share with you. I do not mean that you should disbelieve it because, you see, that is the other side of the leaf; this is the same stuff. It is just the other side of the same stuff. People who disbelieve things know as much about them as people who believe them, which is usually not very much. Whatever you believe you do not know very much about, and whatever you disbelieve you do not know very much about, because belief is a level of certainty which does not necessarily have very much to do with real certainty. Yet the belief level of certainty is the one on which we almost invariably operate; it is the way human beings function. For example, our system of perception – the physiological business of seeing, hearing, smelling and so on – is tied into the level called 'belief'. We know that people are unable to see certain things given their beliefs. In other words, if I do not believe that you are there I may not be able to see you. Or one can produce negative hallucinations under hypnosis, which is itself a function of belief. Any good hypnotist recognizes hypnosis as being grounded in belief. But even in hypnosis belief works both ways. If you do not believe in hypnosis, or have a very strong belief against it, that is often as powerful as believing in it very strongly.

One of the things that Cleve Backster shared with us during the residential conference was a quotation from Max Planck to the effect that science may advance by the death of those people who oppose new theories. There is certainly some truth in that because, as we know, science is very slow to accept new concepts. However, it seems very clear to me that science is slow to accept new ideas because science actually works on a set of beliefs. It itself functions at the level of belief.

So, therefore, do not *believe* anything I say, and by the same token please do not feel it necessary to *disbelieve* what I say. Simply do not worry about whether it is believable or not. Let us imagine that what I am presenting is a novel, and we will see whether it has held together when we get to the end. I would like to share something with you which is incredibly abstract. Unfortunately, if you tell people what you are going to do is abstract, they are bothered because they do not want to be bothered by all those abstractions. But I am using the term in a different way than we normally use it. Normally when we say 'abstraction' we mean an explanation of something. However, what I mean by 'abstraction' is something which precedes what we normally call experience. For instance, if I meet someone for the first time, I have a feeling about her and perhaps she has a feeling about me. But there is something which precedes the feeling. There is something which precedes my attitude about her. There is something that precedes my thoughts about her. There is something that precedes the sensations in my body in relation to her. There is something that precedes my behaviour in relation to her, and that something is that part of experience which exists before the time-space continuum called an abstraction. I would like to talk to you about something which, when compared to the other things that have been talked about this week, is ridiculously simple. By the same token, like all ridiculously simple things, it can get to be very difficult. The simpler it gets, the more difficult it gets at times. The simple thing I would like to talk about is called reality. To make it a little bit more personal, I want to ask you individually how you differentiate between what is real and what is not real. I am not asking what is true. For most people God and truth are purely conceptual. You say 'God' to the average person, and it evokes a picture of a white man with long white hair and a white robe sitting on a white throne with light behind him, despite the fact that *she* is *black!* I like to start where it is very simple, even if it is difficult where it is simple. The question of how do you discern the difference between what is real and what is not real seems to me to be a very fundamental question. But when you ask people what is real, they do not know. Some people think they know. In other words, they have a theory about how they differentiate between what is real and what is not real. But if you observe them, they do not actually differentiate in the way they claim they differentiate. All they have is a theory about what is real and what is not real. So when I ask what is real for you – that is, how do you know what is real, how do you distinguish it from what is not real – I am not asking you what the truth is. I do not even want to discuss the truth with somebody who does not know what reality is; that's presumptuous.

So how do you know what is real? If you sit around and struggle with it, some people will say, 'Well, if I experience it, then I know it is real.'

If I stand up here and I have the sense that there is a bear behind me – you know, I feel I experience that there is a bear behind me – does it mean that there is really a bear back there? In other words, if I feel that there is a bear, if I experience that there is a bear, am I going to be bitten necessarily? The answer to that is obviously 'No'. So the truth of the matter is that you do not differentiate reality from unreality with your feelings. A lot of people say they do, but they do not because nobody has ever been bitten by a bear that they felt sure was there! And until somebody has been bitten by a bear that they feel is there, I have to say that the matter of discerning reality is not a function of one's feelings or experience.

It is something else. The initial test for reality is anything. I mean by that that anything will do as an initial test for reality. Anything *might* be happening. If I feel that there is a bear behind me, there might be – that is an initial test. Or if I am told there is a bear behind me, there might be – that is an initial test. Or if I think there is a bear behind me, there might be, and so on. Almost anything will serve.

Next there is the interim test, the one before the end. The

test before the end for reality is 'reasonableness'. In other words, you and I will act as if things are real to the degree that they are reasonable. In other words, we are likely to behave as though that which is reasonable is real. Reasonableness has many different forms. For instance, one of the forms of reasonableness is a thing called belief. Now beliefs do not have to be very reasonable outside of themselves. As long as they are internally consistent, that is fine. For instance, if you believe that if you stamp your foor four times it rains, and if your system – your data regarding that notion – is consistent with that notion, then that is your belief. You know that every time you stamp your foot four times it rains – except if you do not do it right! But whenever you do it right, it rains. Now somebody standing outside your system says, 'Why, that's crazy! There is no relationship between the rain and your foot stamping.' You say, 'Sure there is.' So let us be clear that reasonableness has many forms, one form of which is belief.

Another form of reasonableness is called logic. Logic is a system of beliefs that has been widely agreed on and formalized. But logic has no more relationship to the truth than any other belief system. A logic system is something that hangs together and cleverly excludes contrary information by explaining it away because it does not fit.

Yet another system of reasonableness is called repetition. If something happens repeatedly, it begins to have some reality for us. We begin to say that is so, that is really real. The same goes for consensus and for authority. Authority is a very interesting form of reasonableness. An authority makes things real for us, not ultimately in fact, but in the interim. So the interim test for reality is reasonableness, and it has many forms – consensus, logic, belief, repetition, authority – and you can probably think of many other things that could go into that list as forms of reasonableness. But what is the ultimate test for reality? What is actually really real for people? If you ask that question, you get an incredible array of answers. People will say, 'Well, what I believe is real is real.' But if you show them that even if the solid wall is there, they cannot walk through it, then somebody will suggest, 'A hallucination produced under hypnosis; if I

believe there is a pillar there, I will walk around the pillar.'
And I have to admit that it might be so, but I also have to
tell them that I will not accept it. I say that the pillar which
they believe is there will not keep the ceiling from caving in
if it needs the support of the pillar which they believe is there
but is not really there. It gets to be very simple after a while.
If you get very simple-minded and get out of your belief
systems and out of your head and become very observational
– not perceptual, but just kind of being there with things –
you see that the parameters, the boundaries of reality, are
actually very physical. In other words, it is almost as if the
ultimate test of reality is physicalness.

The generation just before this one in the United States was
fascinated by love. Love would solve everything. The first
objection is, of course, that most people know that at least
fifty per cent of the traumatic experiences in their lives
revolve around their love affairs with their parents and other
people. And if you listen to songs and poetry about love, they
are almost all sad. So I have a hard time understanding how
people can think that love is going to solve the problems of
the world. But let us assume that love does have this
incredible power and that I love you – though I never act as
if I do. As a matter of fact, every time I see you I hit you on
the head. I wonder how the fact that I love you is very real
for you if I hit you on the head every time I see you. I can
remember my mother giving me a terrible spanking and
telling me she did it because she loved me. I want you to
know that her love for me was not very real. In these ways
life is very much moulded, kind of held in by physical
limitations. We can do a lot of things out of fancy, and in
our thinking we can get very far out, but our actual life
seems to be limited by what is physically real. When people
say, 'Show me,' they are asking for a physical manifestation.
Let us see you make a tumour disappear. Let us see the
tumour disappear. And if you can make enough tumours
disappear, you come to be thought of as a person who
perhaps knows something about cancer. But if you just know
things about cancer and know how tumours disappear, we
are not really very convinced that you know anything real
about cancer.

Real life is actually like that. But it is difficult to accept that. Most wars are fought for very honourable reasons, because people do not understand that dead men do not care. You see, when you are dead, you are dead. That is it. If you died for honourable reasons, you are as dead as if you died for dishonourable reasons! And it is very hard for people who play war to understand that. They think that if you die for honourable reasons, it is a more honourable death. Well death is neither honourable nor dishonourable. It is just death. It is just the way it is. You try going out into the street, and as the bus bears down upon you, you say, 'I don't believe in buses,' and see what happens.

There is another way of looking at it. Alan Watts said that perhaps we were tubes, and that life was putting stuff in at one end of the tube and taking it out at the other. Appendages, arms and legs and a head with a brain inside, were only to make it easier to push stuff in at one end and take it out at the other. People say, 'Well, that is terrible.' But I ask, did you wake up this morning because it was another grand and glorious day or did you wake up because you had to go to the bathroom and had to eat? It was probably because you had to go to the bathroom and eat; and after you had finished going to the bathroom and eating, then you got to the day's business, which of course you interrupted whenever you had to go to the bathroom and eat! And after you had gone to the bathroom and eaten you went back to the day's business until you had to go to the bathroom and eat again. Then, when you went home, you went to the bathroom and ate. Then, after spending the evening going to the bathroom and eating from time to time, you got so tired of going to the bathroom and eating that you went to sleep! Then you wake up the next morning and start the process all over again.

Actually, it is possible to describe the world in terms of going to the bathroom and eating. This may be simplistic. But the point is that we are severely limited by physicalness. After all of this, someone will say, 'Yeah, but how about the guys who walk across fire? What about them?' But again, people always look at the bottoms of the feet of fire-walkers to find out if they really did it, and that is a 'physical' test. We say that fire-walking is possible if you do not burn your feet, which seems to be very physical to me. Nobody sits around thinking about whether fire-walkers actually walk on fire. Ultimately, one looks at the bottom of their feet. Similarly, if a person performs a healing, we want to see some manifestation. Our ultimate test for whether the person really healed a patient is physical, and the ultimate test for almost anything at all in human experience is physicalness. As I said with love, if the person does not act as if they love you, if there is no visible expression of love, you wonder whether they do love you. You start thinking that maybe it is only conceptual, maybe it is not real.

I would like now to get down underneath reasonableness and see what reasonableness is. Of what stuff is reasonableness composed? First, it has many forms. In other words, it has the form of belief, it has the form of logic, it has the form of consensus, it has the form of authority, it has the form of repetition. It has many forms. But what is the substance of those forms? In other words, of what is that stuff composed? What is reasonableness in substance? Not what is it in form, because in form this, for instance, is a blackboard – in substance it is particles or waves. So what is the substance of reasonableness?

If you take a good look at the problem, you find that there is a repeated pattern in each one of these forms. In other words, there is something which happens every time you take a look at one of those forms, and that keeps happening every time you take a look at one of those forms. It is called agreement. In other words, the actual substance of reasonableness is agreement. If you take a look at any one of reasonableness's forms, you find the substance called agreement. A belief system is that which agrees with itself, a logic system is that which agrees with itself. Consensus is obviously agreement and repetition is also something which happens in an agreeable way one time after another. Authority too is established by agreement. We say that if a person has done this, this and this, he is an authority in his field. It does not make much difference whether he knows anything about it – so long as he has done this, this and this, he is an authority. We also establish authority by voting. We say, 'How many people think that this person is an authority?' Everybody puts their hands up, so again we get authority by agreement. So if you look at reasonableness, you see very clearly that reasonableness is actually a function of agreement. If this is so, what is real for you and me is a function of agreement and then ultimately what is real for you and me is a function of physicalness – rather than just that stuff called agreement.

So let us take a look at physicalness and see if we can get down to the substance of physicalness. What is physicalness? If you sit around and think about it for a long time, and argue about it and take a look at your arguments, you finally get to see that physicalness is actually a substance called measurability. If you can measure it, then it is real, and if you cannot measure it, it is not. What do I mean by 'measure'? Well, to measure something means to be able to note a beginning, a middle and an end. For those people who want to split hairs, you only have to note one of those. You can infer the other two. But you do have to be able to note one of them. Something which does not have a beginning or a middle or an end is not measurable: you cannot measure it.

Now let us take a closer look at that theory and see if it holds water. I would like you to imagine what we call that sound which does not have any beginning, middle or end. In other words, what do we call a sound that is always there? It is called silence. Silence is the experience of the absence of any beginning, middle or end of sound. If we are all completely quiet, there is no way of knowing whether there is any sound or not – if it does not have a beginning, a middle or an end. Similarly, if you took this piece of chalk and extended it infinitely in all directions so that it had no starting place – no place where it started – it would become space. Whatever does not have a beginning or an end, which means it is not measurable, is necessarily not physical. If it is physical, it is measurable because that is what physicalness is. Physicalness is a function of measurability.

What we are really asking here is what is the substance of beginningness or endingness or middleness? What is the substance of that stuff? What is it that says that this thing begins here? Now, this appears to be incredibly abstract! But it is not so abstract that you cannot see it. If you look at a blackboard, you say and I say that the board begins right here at its edge. But we say that because we have the agreement of the absence of the board. We do not say that the board begins over *here*, because we do not have that agreement that the board begins beyond its edge; but everybody agrees that it begins here at its edge. So you have got a kind of conspiracy. The conspiracy about matter is an absolute and total conspiracy among human beings. In other words, then, whenever you have a total agreement that something is so, you call that physicalness. Everything in the entire universe – that is, everything in the physical universe – agrees that this board begins at its edge. Nothing argues against it. And so we could say that both the interim test of reality is agreement and the ultimate test of reality is agreement. We could say that everything which really exists is a function of agreement. So the true substance of reality is agreement and what is totally and absolutely real – that is that physical stuff – is totally and absolutely real because it is totally and absolutely agreed by everyone and everything. Everyone and everything acts as if it is there. Every once in a while, of course, you get someone who seems to transcend that agreement and then you have a kind of breakdown of reality. Reality starts to break down when you see and hear some of the things that you have seen and heard this week. But essentially it is still very solid; it is very persistent, which by the way is the quality of reality. Reality is solid and persistent – that is its quality – and its substance is agreement and its forms are reasonableness and physicalness. Now let us move on to another seemingly abstract idea. When you look at reality, what do you look with? What is the set of all sets about reality which people have? What is the place we come *from* about reality? In science you try to find out something so that you can make a general statement, a generalization embracing numbers of examples or facts. For example, if you know that a blackboard is black and that is all you know, it is not very interesting. But if you think you know that all boards are black, you may have found out something interesting. You can then verify whether all boards are black by studying this one and then generalizing. As long as the blackboard is there and you know it, you have been confirmed. But when something does not fit, then you have been invalidated.

Now we will turn to some science of philosophy. Generally, we want science to help to explain the whole universe, which is a very difficult subject for either science or philosophy. So we will use a scientific method to discuss the universe. The scientific method for studying something that is too big to study is to make a model – an analogue – of it. So we need an analogue of the universe, which is a great problem just in itself, but we will try it anyhow.

First of all, to make a model of the universe, you have to define it – so I am going to define the universe. The universe is a bunch of stuff happening. That is not a bad definition. I do not know how useful it is – we will find out – but at least it is not a static definition; it does fit – the universe is a bunch of stuff happening. That is observable; you can test it out. Now we are going to set up an analogue – we are going to make something happen. If I shove this lady, you know what will happen. She will fall over and she will hit that gentleman and when he gets hit he will fall over and he will hit the next person, and when she gets hit she will fall over – and that is our model of the universe. It is a lot of stuff happening.

Good scientific methodology requires you to frame the multi-faceted event and study one event at a time, the essential event. So we are going to frame this last person who will fall over into the aisle because there is no one else to fall up against. If we put a frame around that event, what we see when we look into the frame is a person falling into the aisle. No, we will make it a little wider. The gentleman hits the lady and then she falls into the aisle.

Now the philosophy and the philosophical question is this: is that lady an effect or a cause? If you think about it, if you get very philosophical about it, she is first one, then she is the other, and then she is both. But if you are simple-minded about it, she is obviously an effect. She fell over; so that is an effect.

Now our generalization from our little scientific study is that the universe is composed of effects. But if we go out and publish papers saying this, people will start screaming and hollering in the streets that it is nonsense – that everybody knows you cannot only have effects. If I tell you that the universe is composed of effects alone, it will bother you. Have you noticed nobody likes that? So I say, all right, there is something wrong with my methodology, I will expand the frame and I will take another look. If we expand the frame, we find that this gentleman bashes into this lady and she falls over. Now we have the lady as an effect and the man as a cause. So now we generalize and say the universe is full of causes and effects, and everybody feels great. The experimentation and the generalization have now become acceptable because they fit your ground of being. If I tell you that the universe is full of effects alone, you will object because your ground of being says that is not true. Your ground of being says that the universe is a cause and effect system, and if there is an effect, there had better be a cause, and if there is a cause there had better be an effect.

If you look up the word 'cause' in the dictionary, it has a circular definition with the word 'effect'. When you look up 'cause', it says 'that which gives off effects'. If you look up 'effect', it says 'that which comes out of a cause'. This is the ground of being of our existence, of the universe. Yet if we call this gentlemen a cause, a large problem arises – while it satisfies our ground of being, while we all feel all right walking around assigning causes to effects and effects to causes, it does not work at all well when you begin to actually observe what happens. If we again expand the frame, we find out that the gentlemen is not a cause at all, he is an effect. A lady knocked him over. Now we have found the real cause and everybody feels great again; except when we examine this cause, we find it is not actually a cause, it is an effect. I was the one who set things in motion. You say, well, now we have found the real cause. But I am not actually the cause either, because when I was a little boy my mother was bad to me and that is why I go round knocking ladies around, so my mother is actually the cause. But, of course, she cannot be the cause either, because she was only bad to me because my father was bad to her. And it goes on for ever and ever. Every time you examine a cause carefully, it is always an effect.

This leads us to an almost untenable position – reality is effect alone. Everything comes out of everything else, which came out of everything else, which came out of everything else, which came out of everything else. And mind you, that is pretty much what the physicists have said. Physics is that branch of science which studies Chinese boxes. A Chinese box is an object which, when you open it, has another box inside it. If you open that box, there is yet another box. You open that box, and find another box. Open that box, and there is yet another box. I have a scorecard on which I keep track of particles that the physicists get when they break particles apart, and they keep on getting more particles when they break particles apart. I just hang around physics without understanding at all. I do not understand mathematics either. However, you do not have to be a mathematician to understand physics, as Einstein proved. I like physics, so I try to hang around physicists. They say the most incredible things that do not make any sense at all. For example, they say that things are two different things at the same time, or not, depending on how you look at them, and that depends on what is good for you! You are not supposed to say things like that if you are a physicist. Then I found out that there were junior physicists and senior physicists, and the senior physicists are allowed to say such things while the junior physicists are not.

Let us recap. If I keep saying it over and over again, it begins to get a little bit more real; and that is almost as good a technique as proving it! I mean, what is the difference? It is still a function of agreement. If I prove that what I have said is true, all I will have done is to amass an army of agreeing facts. And if I say it over and over and over and over again, what have I done? I have amassed an army of agreeing statements. What is the difference?

The agony is almost over.

To review very quickly, we could say that reality interimly is a function of reasonableness and ultimately is a function of physicalness; and that we are hemmed in and moulded interimly by reasonableness and ultimately by physicalness. Furthermore, when you look at the substance of reasonableness, it becomes agreement, and when you look at the substance of physicalness, it becomes measurability which is ultimately agreement. So what follows from this is that the ultimate substance end-test for reality is agreement alone. When you have total agreement you have what is called total reality. When you have almost total agreement you have a lot of reality. When you do not have much agreement, you have not got much reality. And, by the way, disagreement works just as well as agreement because disagreement is like agreement. You see, you cannot really disagree with anything you have not already agreed with, unless you have no position at all in the matter. For example, would you agree that there are pink elephants in this room? No, you probably would not. Then my question is: why are you thinking about pink elephants? Well, you are thinking about pink elephants because they became a little real for you. You see, you then disagree. In order to disagree however, you had to have the notion of what a pink elephant in a room looks like and had to look around and see that there were not any pink elephants. Now, most of you are actually not quite that experiential. You figured it out.

At any rate, that is one way of looking at things. But it is only half the story. We have still to take a look at the other half of the story. The other half of the story is the question about what is unreal. The question I am asking is: what is unreality in terms of unreality? In other words, does anything exist which is not a function of agreement? Is there a ceiling above you – even though it is not being experienced by you? As a matter of fact, even if you looked up there you cannot 'experience the ceiling'. The theory about sight is that there is an electrochemical change in your visual cortex, so the only information you are getting from the ceiling, even theoretically, is an electrochemical change in your visual cortex. Now how many people are experiencing electro-chemical change in their visual cortex? Nobody is. First of all, most of us do not even know we have a visual cortex; I mean not experientially. We only know it theoretically. So when you look up at the ceiling, it is true that you have the experience of the ceiling, but it is not true that you are experiencing the ceiling. The ceiling that you are actually experiencing is the one in your eye or your brain. At any rate, when you take a look at unreality, unreality is also actually composed of experience. It is experience without any agreement and without any disagreement. It has not yet taken on a form. It has not yet got into the system called reality.

It is interesting to note that experience is in fact non-physical. For instance, if I ask you where you are experiencing me, you will probably point somewhere in the direction of your body. If I ask you where I am, you will point somewhere in the direction of my body. Then I have to ask you, 'Well, if I'm over here and you're over there, and the experience is over there, you must be experiencing you because you are over there and not me. I'm over here. As a matter of fact, you may only be experiencing you.' The agreement is, the alleged reality is, that you are experiencing me because I am out here. But as a matter of fact you are actually experiencing you. The form of the experience is the agreement, this stuff out here, but the experience itself is over there. Now the problem with talking about experience being over there is that when you go to locate the exact point of experience, you cannot do it. Most people will say, 'Oh, it is up here in the head.' That is because they think it is up here. But if in fact you take a look – do not think about or believe where you experience, but look at where you are experiencing me – you actually cannot find any place where you experience me because experience does not happen in any place. It happens somewhere that is not measurable. Experience is not measurable; only distance between event or object is measurable. A physicist cleared that up for me by explaining that space is abstract, totally, which means that it is only experiential. You can experience space, but you cannot measure it. When you measure it, it becomes distance. The point I am making is that experience does not happen in some place. Nor does it happen at some time. Everybody talks about 'here and now', but 'here and now' is not some time. There is no now; no time called now. There is an experience called now, but no time called now. The instant you try to make some time out of it, it becomes then; it is never now. So now is experiential. Time is experiential, space is experiential and substance is experiential. Form is non-experiential. Form is the stuff over here you see, but the substance of experience does not happen out in the space-time-form continuum. It happens experientially – which is not in some place, which is not at some time and which does not have any form.

So what is left? One thing is body sensations, feelings in our emotional system, attitudes in our mental system, behaviour in our kinaesthetic or muscular system, thoughts and perhaps even memories; they are a fall-out of the actual experience which is totally abstract, which is a substance without form. One of the real points that I wanted to make is that if you will take a look at this, you see that experience has no effect. It is only cause. A person looks for the source of their experience outside themselves because most people think that this is where experience happens. But if, in fact, you become clear, and it is possible to become clear about this, you see that experience is a function of self – that self *is* experience, not the form of experience. Body is form. Emotion is form. Personality is form. I call my particular form Werner Erhard, but I am not Werner Erhard. I am that which precedes all those forms, the experience itself. It does not have any antecedents. It starts right there, and it is a kind of system of responsibility which makes you responsible for everything you experience. It does not, however, make you responsible for reality, except in a very ultimate and first-cause way. You see, if I experience love, if I have that experience, then it manifests according to the laws of agreement of reality, but the love itself starts out as an experience.

By the way, these two words reality and unreality are obviously intermixed. We call that which is only conceptual and exists only by agreement reality, and that which is only experiential unreality. I do not think this is right. I will change this and call our experience reality, and agreement illusion. By the way, illusions are not the things you think they are. Most people think illusions are very non-expressible. But, actually, illusions are solid and persistent. People refuse to recognize that. Illusions are solid and persistent; reality has no persistence. It does not even exist in time. It does not have a form. You have to have a form to persist. Reality is nowhere.

The final point I want to make is that to the degree that what I am saying is consistent with people, in other words, to the degree that it illuminates the condition called life, to the degree that it gives some sense to the condition called living – in other words, the degree to which it is valid – it assigns cause for our experience with us alone. What I am saying recognizes that once you have created an experience, it then becomes, and goes out of your hands into the system of agreements, taking its course in that system of agreements. However, once you understand that, it is possible to reverse the process back to the original experience. Then an incredible thing happens – you experience what you have experienced.

I am not going to tell you what I think happens because it would take too long. I am going to stop here and wrap this thing up.

I want to be very clear with you that I did not tell you any of this because I wanted you to believe it. I do not think it is believable. I did not tell it to you because I wanted your approval of it. It is perfectly all right with me if you do not either agree or disagree, approve or disapprove. It does not make it any more, or any less, the truth whether you agree with it or disagree with it. It is the truth to the degree that it is, and it is not to the degree that it is not. My notion is that all systems of the truth are interim anyhow, because the truth actually rests here in a person's experience.

I have found it incredibly valuable in my own personal life, in my own experience, to be able to differentiate between my things and myself. I found it incredibly valuable to be able to take total and absolute responsibility – and I mean those words exactly the way I said them – total and absolute responsibility for my own personal experience, and to be able to give you the space to take total and absolute responsibility for your own personal experience – to understand that in the matter of agreements you have responsibilities and that you have entered into those agreements. I have agreed that buses run people over and to that degree I have a responsibility to get myself out of the way or suffer the consequences. It is a very, very interesting thing. This thing, this approach, is kind of mind-blowing because it is unsystematic. It constantly argues with itself. It is paradoxical. It is nonsensical. I say this about the truth; for me the truth does not make any sense at all, given our realities. I am now arguing for nonsense, that we ought to embrace all nonsense. That would be merely reaction, you know. I am saying that perhaps we ought to apply some other criteria, some other measurement to the truth, than we currently do.

My own personal measurement for the truth, and I share it with you, is satisfaction. Does this way of being in the world enable me to experience completion in my life? Does it enable me to experience satisfaction in my life? Or do I keep needing more to be all right? Or do I alternatively experience where I am right now to be sufficient right now? Not for tomorrow, mark you, but for right now. That is my kind of measuring step. In a more poetic form, I call it aliveness, and I am bold enough to think that I really do not need to define it for you because I think everybody knows the experience I am talking about without my defining it. But at any rate, so that we can at least talk about it, my label for it is happiness, health, love and self-expression. These are the ways I measure the validity of this thing.

The May Lectures: An Overview

The May Lectures was 'covered' by a number of journalists, but few took on the task of comprehensively assessing the diverse material which was presented. Stuart Holroyd was commissioned by *BRES,* a journal published in the Netherlands. His accounts have been published by *BRES* in Dutch but appear here, in substantially the same form, in English. Holroyd's material is, to some extent, duplicative, but the duplication is worth it; first because the subjects are complex and occasionally arcane and second because his insights are incisive and his writing lucid.

THE MAY LECTURES
Stuart Holroyd

On Health and Healing and 'Bioenergetics'

There are always men and women working at the frontiers of knowledge, suffering the derision and the opprobrium of their peers, patiently pursuing their researches, biding their time. When fifty of them come together to exchange ideas and to pool the results of their researches, and when they can draw a paying audience of some eight hundred people every evening for a week to listen to them, they might justifiably feel that at last their time has come.

This is what happened in London in May 1974. Fifty scientists from Britain, Canada and the United States spent a week in closed conference at Brunel University, and in the evenings fourteen of them gave public lectures in a large theatre in the centre of the city. The general title of the seminar and the lecture series was 'New Approaches to Health and Healing, Individual and Social'. It was a modest and tentative title for a series of talks in which we were asked to believe,. among other things, that plants can read a man's mind and can be responsive to human emotion at a distance of seven hundred miles, that psychic surgery can remove diseased parts of internal organs without anaesthetic and without cutting the skin, that a man can learn to control and even to stop the beating of his heart and the flow of his blood, that material objects can be transported over a distance of six thousand miles by the power of the mind, and that Mr Uri Geller's paranormal powers are the gift of extra-terrestrial beings who are using him as a witness to their existence and as a precursor to their manifesting themselves to mankind.

I say that we were asked to believe these things, but it would be more accurate to say that we were either shown them or told them. The scientific rigour and thoroughness of some of the demonstrations was impressive. Here was scientific rationalism pursuing its methodology to the point where it called in question its own foundations. For four centuries scientific-rational man has pursued Sir Francis Bacon's programme of extending man's sovereignty over Nature, only to discover in these latter days that he is not sovereign but subject, that Nature does not serve him but rather he serves Nature, that a scientific and philosophical method based upon systematic doubt does not lead to ultimate knowledge but to perplexity and paralysis in the face of the mysteries of man, Nature and the cosmos, and the greater mystery of their interrelations. We are all heirs to scientific rationalism. We seek knowledge by applying principles of measure and verification. We are not naively credulous. But more and more of us these days are turning from the philosophical question 'How can we know?' to the question 'What can we know?'; from epistemology to metaphysics; from a method not based upon doubt but upon openness, a willingness to suspend disbelief, and perhaps even ultimately upon faith. We may find it difficult to believe in Mr Uri Geller's powers of materialization and in his extra-terrestrial controls, but

when we have seen irrefutable evidence that plants 'think'
and that 'psychic surgery' works we cannot peremptorily
dismiss such claims because they are improbable and
unproven; we can only suspend disbelief.

As some of the topics that will arise are controversial and
demand a reappraisal of prevailing ideas about man, Nature,
health and healing, I think that it is appropriate for me first
to present my credentials and declare my interests. I am not
trained in any scientific discipline. My subjects are literature
and philosophy. My first book, published sixteen years ago,
was about varieties of religious experience as expressed in
modern poetry. My interests, literary and philosophical, have
always been in the area of what we might broadly call the
religious or spiritual, in man's relation to the transcendent,
in the potentialities of human growth and the methods and
disciplines through which it might be pursued. On the other
hand, I have always been sceptical of spiritualism, occultism
and concern with psychic phenomena because I have always
considered that man tends to be more concerned with the
fixation of belief than with the pursuit of knowledge, and
that spiritualism and occultism as beliefs are narrow, impoverished, escapist and dangerous. To regard them as areas
worthy of research and inquiry is a different matter. I have
followed researches into E.S.P. and psychic phenomena over
the years with interest. I have not particularly been an
enthusiast, however, because I have not seen how, even if all
the claims of the spiritualists, the occultists and the psychics
were proved true, this would in any way affect the world we
live in and the way we live.

The May Lectures have caused me to have second thoughts
on this latter assumption. The ground covered was a fraction
of the area currently designated 'paranormal', but if the
claims of these lecturers alone are true, the implications for
our philosophy of man and Nature and for our approach to
health and healing, to religion and to interpersonal relationships are revolutionary.

A revolution can be a turning upside down or a turning full
circle, a returning to origins. There is ancient wisdom; there
is forgotten, or half-remembered, knowledge. We live in
thought-pockets, culture-pockets, under orthodoxies and

rituals that circumscribe life and make it intelligible. Man seeks the fixation of belief, the settlement of opinion. No civilization was ever built upon doubt and perplexity. Man sees himself as a creature flung into the flux of time, and as such his primary need is not to be but to do. He must be active, and to be so he needs certainties. But the certainties of one culture may be the doubts of another, and in times when his certainties and orthodoxies have run man into an impasse and up against problems he can no longer cope with, he may begin to look elsewhere, to other times and other cultures, for a truth, a method, a philosophy to act upon and to live by.

And he may begin to look more closely at himself. Every civilization functions on the basis of certain assumptions about man, about the nature and the responsibilities of his relations to others and to his society, and about the way in which he achieves his optimum personal development and fulfilment. Though ours is still nominally a Christian society, there are few people who would argue that a religious view of man prevails in our institutions, our relationships, our values and our idea of the good life. We are all progeny of industrialism, producers and consumers all. We are powerfully and invidiously influenced to adopt a mechanistic philosophy of man.

This mechanistic philosophy has found its way into commonly accepted attitudes to health and healing. People tend to think of the body as a kind of machine that can go wrong, and to think that when it goes wrong, it should be put into the hands of specialist doctors rather in the way that we put a car into a garage when it has to be repaired. Health is thought of as a commodity that can be bought and sold. Ours is a civilization entranced by the wonders of technology, and people tend to put their faith in the fact that medical technology can achieve wonders comparable with space technology. 'Spare-part surgery' is always news, and not long ago a successful practitioner achieved international fame reminiscent of that of the matinee idols of the films of the nineteen-thirties. It is indeed a marvellous technological achievement to successfully transplant a heart, but at the same time it is rather like putting a new engine in a motor car, and for such surgery to be publicized as the peak achievement of medical science does tend to reinforce the mechanistic concept of the human body and the idea that when one of its functions goes wrong, we are entirely dependent upon the expertise of a 'specialist'.

That we need fundamentally to rethink our paradigm of health and our ideas of the functions of doctors and hospitals in our society was the argument of the opening speaker in the May Lectures series, Mr Rick Carlson. Mr Carlson, an American lawyer with a professed special interest in 'the delivery of health care and of legal services', argued provocatively – as was appropriate for an opening speaker – that our society has too much medical care, that our medical system is no longer producing health but is causing more ills than it cures. It is a system concerned with medicine, not with health, with curing rather than with preventing disease, with symptoms rather than with fundamental causes. And it does not work. White male longevity in the United States is actually decreasing.

Yet at the same time, more and more money is spent every year on medical care. Regarded in the cold light of statistical and commercial considerations, it is an investment producing diminishing returns. Why? The question has to be asked. The pharmaceutical industry will not ask it. They have a vested interest in allopathic medicine – the treatment of symptoms by means of drugs and surgery. But the public at large, and responsible doctors particularly, should ask it. Are there not alternatives to allopathic medicine? Is to combat disease the same thing as to produce health? Is disease itself to be construed merely as a malfunction of the human organism? What is the part played by social and environmental factors and by a person's lifestyle in producing disease? To what extent does the availability of medical resources dictate the amount of sickness in a society? What concept of man, of his functions and his capacities, underlies prevailing attitudes to health and healing? These are questions that are not being asked and investigated; no doubt because if they were investigated their answers would demand radical changes in the present system.

Science and philosophy have come together in recent years in adopting a 'holistic' approach to the understanding of man and of Nature. The 'divide and conquer' approach of rationalistic science, the demarcation of separate areas of specialization, the regarding of moral and philosophical considerations as irrelevant to the pursuit of pure scientific research, and the tendency of accomplished technocrats to regard themselves as an elite and create around themselves a protective mystique: these are some of the factors that have led orthodox science into an impasse, that have caused it to create more problems than it has solved. But all this is changing. The mood, the methods, the underlying assumptions are changing. Ecology, the science of interactions and interdependence of living systems, has in recent years become a matter of public concern and public debate. Humanistic psychology, developing from the pioneer work of Abraham Maslow, and focusing scientific method not on means of treating mental illness but on means of promoting mental health and the optimum growth and development of the human being, has not only become 'respectable' in the United States but has infiltrated the institutions and been applied practically by great industrial corporations. These are examples of the 'holistic' approach, the study of the functioning of wholes rather than of parts, the emphasis on life as process and interaction. But this 'holistic' philosophy of man and Nature has not yet influenced that area of science that most widely and intimately touches upon our everyday lives, namely medical science. If health were regarded as a process and not as a static condition, the implications for medical science would be immense. It is well established by now that there is nothing static in Nature, that stasis in fact is death, and yet people still tend to think of disease in a human being as a falling away from a fixed norm of health and to believe that a cure can reinstate the norm. But to return an organism to a condition of precarious stasis is no cure. For a man whose lifestyle has given him stomach ulcers to have the offending ulcers removed surgically and then to return to the lifestyle that produced them is no strategy for producing health. Health must be regarded as a dynamic not a static condition, not as a property or birthright of a human being but as a condition intimately bound up with his employment of his energies, his way of functioning within his environment, and even with his sense of personal identity and personal evolution. To regard it thus would be to adopt a 'holistic' approach to health.

An immediate result of the adoption of such an approach would be a cut-back in allopathic medicine, a reduction of dependence on the symbols of healing, on the services of specialists, hospitals and all the paraphernalia of medical technology. People would develop a more positive and responsible attitude to the maintenance of their own health. They would still fall sick and contract diseases, but they would experience their sickness and would learn about the body and its functions by consciously combating pain and disease. We have all heard stories of miraculous self-cures, of cancer patients pronounced incurable by doctors who have simply refused to die and have mysteriously rid themselves of the malignancy. Such things are well substantiated, and to regard them as miracles and mysteries inaccessible to man's science and understanding is surely short-sighted and may even be considered irresponsible and unscientific. A 'holistic' approach to health and healing would investigate such phenomena, would seek to explore and measure the relationship and interactions between mind and body and between man and Nature. This, in fact, is precisely the type of investigative work that many of the scientists and doctors who contributed to the May Lectures in London have been engaged on. Their collective testimony gives us reason to hope that in the years ahead 'holistic' medicine may make inroads into the institutions comparable to those being made today by its companion science, humanistic psychology.

It takes a long time to change entrenched and institutionalized concepts and attitudes. Western philosophy, religion and science are all based on dualistic concepts. Mind and body, spirit and matter, conscious man and unconscious Nature, have in our civilization been regarded as irreconcilable opposites. Industrialism and technology are based upon dualistic concepts, on the idea of man using, exploiting and controlling Nature and natural forces. Eastern civilizations, which have always been based upon an organic, unitive view of the universe, have not developed technologically.

For more than two millennia East and West have gone their separate ways. But in the twentieth century there has been a gradual convergence. Relativity theory established that mass is equivalent to energy, and quantum field theory further showed that mass is not an intrinsic property of matter but arises from a particle's interaction with its environment or 'field'. A part of the environment in any physical experiment is always the experimenter himself, and thus, as the physicist Werner Heisenberg wrote, 'natural science does not simply describe and explain nature; it is a part of the interplay between nature and ourselves.' Relativity and quantum theory demolished the dualistic foundations of Western philosophy and science decades ago and sketched a model of the cosmogony as a process of interaction and energy exchange that has striking correspondences with Eastern philosophies. It did not take long for man to employ these principles destructively. He developed the nuclear fission bomb thirty years ago. But it is only now, and only very gradually, that the positive implications of modern theoretical physics are being seen and applied.

'Energy' is a key term in the new philosophy and science. We have come a long way since Einstein showed that mass is energy. The distinguished Russian astrophysicist, Dr Nikolai Kozyrev, has recently put forward the hypothesis that time is a form of energy, and his recondite researches and reasoning have been received with excitement by Western physicists. Less hypothetical at this stage is the idea that 'psychic energy' and 'bioenergetic systems' exist and play an important part in our lives, a part which is becoming increasingly important as scientists evolve means of observing, checking and measuring them at work. 'Bioenergetics' and 'psychoenergetics' are neologisms for new scientific disciplines. And they are literally disciplines, in the sense that they apply strict scientific methods of checking and measuring to the phenomena they study. This has only recently become possible, with the development of sophisticated and sensitive electronic equipment like the electroencephalograph, the polygraph, the tobiscope, biofeedback machines and the Kirlian photographic process. With the aid of such equipment it is now possible to observe and monitor the energy systems of living organisms, and as research is being pursued it is becoming increasingly clear that these energy systems are not discrete and separate entities but are interconnected and interresponsive. The perennial intuition of poets and mystics that 'all life is one' is no longer an airy abstraction but a hard and proven scientific fact. All life is one, and the principle of its unity is energy exchange between living organisms. Thus biological research parallels and endorses quantum field theory. Not only matter, but thought too, is energy. And with the establishment of this principle as scientific fact many phenomena hitherto regarded as occult or supernatural become at once both more credible and more accessible to scientific investigation – for example, telepathy, psychokinesis, 'miracle' healing, precognition, and even astrology and the existence of ghosts.

The term 'thought' in the proposition 'thought is a form of energy' can be construed both as 'volition' and as 'cognition'. In other words, we are talking both about willing and about knowing. This is an important distinction, for it not only defines two distinct areas of investigation but also enables us to separate paranormal phenomena into two categories: those that are more easily credible because they are endorsed by fairly common experience and conform to a degree to our existing concepts, and those that seem incredible because they defy interpretation in terms of existing concepts of man, Nature and science. Thought energy as volition is a more acceptable idea to our minds than the idea of thought energy as cognition. We can more readily accept that the will to live can be a positive factor in the cure of cancer than that a plant can 'read' a man's mind when he conceives a destructive intention towards it. We can believe in the power of mind over matter more easily than we can believe that matter itself has some of the properties of mind. And if we investigate why we can more easily believe in it, we will see that the root cause is our ingrained dualistic habits of thought. We conceive of mind as something that differs from body and from matter both in the way it is constituted and in the way it functions. We regard it as being above body and matter and equate it with conscious control, with order and organization. And as we tend to think of energy in terms of motion and change, which are concepts connected with order and organization, it is not difficult for us to accept that volition is a form of energy. Tell people that the will can be a positive factor in effecting a cancer cure and they will probably marvel at the mysterious powers of the mind. But tell them that plants think and they will probably regard you as soft-headed or plain crazy. Yet both of these well-substantiated phenomena probably have something to do with the same root cause, with what has been called 'cellular consciousness'. Thought is a form of energy, but as such it is by no means an exclusive property of the mind and it is certainly not exclusively located in the brain. There is an accumulation of evidence indicating that cognition is a field phenomenon. Blind people have been known to discriminate colours and even to read with their fingers, and deaf people have been taught to hear with the aid of electrical devices attached to the skin. Many other examples could be given of the body performing functions that we normally associate with the mind.

What I have tried to do so far is to adumbrate some of the themes of the May Lectures, to show how they are related, to elucidate some of the terminology employed by scientists researching paranormal phenomena, and to discuss the general philosophical significance and background of these researches. I have suggested that we are witnessing in our time the beginning of a revolution in ways of thinking about man, Nature and life, a revolution that can endow human life with incalculable benefits. Man has always looked to religion, to the arts, to mysticism and to philosophy for that sense of expanded consciousness, that sense of transcending the limits of a self that is located in a particular space and time, that affinity with other lives and other forms of life from which he derives his profoundest satisfactions. A psychology and a medical science based upon a mechanistic philosophy of man and concerned with his effective functioning in a materialistic environment and scheme of values have considered religion, the arts, mysticism and philosophy irrelevant to their function. But now we have humanistic psychology, concerned with spiritual growth; holistic medicine, concerned with the promotion of health rather than the curing of disease; and a range of life sciences which, starting from different points, suggest that, as poets and mystics and the religions of the East have always claimed, all life is ultimately one and that man, Nature and the cosmos are constituted of the same stuff, common to matter, mind and body, and are perennially linked in a continuum of activity and response. The implications are truly revolutionary.

On Volition

The question of the degree of conscious control that man has over his own internal states, his destiny and his environment is one upon which the world's religions and philosophies have always sharply differed. Western philosophers have for centuries debated the question of free will and determinism and today the debate is no less acrimonious than it ever was, though it is conducted in scientific terms rather than religious, with behaviourists maintaining a strict determinism and humanistic psychologists maintaining the efficacy of free will and conscious choice. The argument is so old, so perennial and so bitter that it might be relevant to ask whether it is really an argument over the nature of things or a quarrel between two different types of human being, each with a predisposition or a temperamental need to believe in either determinism or free will. There is a temperament that craves order, submission and a sense of belonging, and that does not find repugnant the idea of an inscrutable Divine Will directing human affairs. Then there is the temperament that craves independence and self-determination, the right consciously to choose and vigorously to pursue its own salvation or damnation. Dostoevsky dramatized the quarrel between the two temperaments in his portrayal of the two Karamazov brothers, Alyosha and Ivan, and it is a recurrent theme in all of his major novels. Tolstoy, in *War and Peace,* inveighed against the Great Man view of history and preached historical determinism, but at the same time portrayed an individual, Pierre, shaping his own destiny through acts of will, choice and intelligence. Literature, as well as philosophy and religion, has got good mileage out of the question of the degree of conscious control that man has over his destiny. And it is a question still very much open to debate; though what has been discovered about volition in other contexts might ultimately be seen to lend support to those who believe at least in a degree of free will.

Western medicine and psychology have been based on the idea that man can exercise very little control over his internal states and bodily functions. The prevailing paradigm of the human being for most scientists is of a creature totally determined by genetic pattern and environmental conditioning. This paradigm has been so prevalent that there has been very little support for research into the possibilities of mind-body self-regulation. But while official science has been cautious, conservative and sceptical, public interest in Eastern religions, yoga and transcendental meditation, as well as in dubious eclectic and hybrid self-regulation techniques such as scientology, has grown apace. The time had to come when 'respectable science' threw caution to the winds and adopted a new approach to the mind-body problem.

A pioneer of this new approach has been Dr Elmer Green, who gave one of the May Lectures in London under the title 'Biofeedback and Voluntary Control of Internal States'. Dr Green is head of the Psychophysiology Laboratory in the Research Department of the Menninger Foundation, and ten years ago he established what he called the 'Voluntary Controls Project' at the Menninger Foundation. His lecture reported on the techniques developed and the discoveries made in the course of his research.

Dr Green does not claim to be an innovator. He points out that as long ago as 1905, Johannes Schultz in Germany began to study different techniques of hypno-therapy combined with the disciplines of yoga. By 1910 he had developed a therapeutic system which he called 'autogenic training'. In this system, patients learned to relax tense muscles and to regulate blood flow and heart rate by using verbal phrases, and eventually to focus their control efforts on specific psychosomatic disorders. The method proved highly successful in curing certain diseases, but it was never widely practised.

Since 1964, Dr Green has been able to follow up Schultz's

work with the aid of sophisticated and highly sensitive electronic equipment.

The idea of 'biofeedback' is basically simple. It is that when a person is provided with immediate knowledge of internal body processes, he can learn to control sections of his physiological machinery that are normally regarded as operating involuntarily.

In a biofeedback research session a subject, sitting comfortably in a chair, has electrodes attached to the back of his head, his right forearm and two fingers of his right hand. He wears a special jacket equipped with a respiration-gauge. An experimenter sits at a control panel behind him and directs the biofeedback training session. The aim is self-regulation of muscle tension, body temperature and brain wave rhythm. The electrodes detect changes in these internal states and relay the information back to the subject by means of three bars of light on a screen in front of him. The bars, like that of a mercury thermometer, become taller or shorter in response to changes in the physiological state that each is monitoring. The subject first aims to achieve complete relaxation, and he can watch the progress of his efforts on the feedback meter wired to the muscle in his forearm. Having achieved this, he concentrates on temperature regulation, and the electrodes attached to his fingers measure his success in raising his body temperature and relay the information to the second bar on the screen. He then endeavours to induce a state of consciousness that produces alpha rhythms in the brain, a state that combines alertness with complete calm. The third bar rises to its maximum height when he succeeds in producing alpha rhythms for a period of ten seconds.

Dr Green, having observed hundreds of sessions of biofeedback training, has some interesting observations on how volition works. He compares it to farming, and remarks that 'there seems to be a correspondence between human physiological responses to volition and the way Nature responds in general to human initiative.' A farmer first desires and visualizes a crop, then plants the seed, then allows Nature to take its course, and finally reaps his crop. Similarly, the biofeedback subject first visualizes a certain kind of physiological behaviour, then plants the idea in the unconscious, or, physiologically speaking, the subcortex of the brain, allows it to develop there without the interference of anxiety or conscious effort, and finally attains the desired physiological result. The correspondence with techniques of meditation as taught in Eastern religions will be obvious to many readers, and some may recall the lines of the modern religious poet T. S. Eliot in *The Rock:*

> I say to you: Make perfect your will.
> I say: take no thought of the harvest,
>   But only of proper sowing.

The poet, the mystics and the scientist concur that for volition to work, a certain state of mind must be induced – a state that is non-anxious, non-interfering, totally calm, a state of 'letting be'. The farmer does not dig up his seeds to see how they are getting on. He initiates the process of growth, then lets Nature take its course. Volition, in the context of the mind-body interrelationship, is analogous. It is not characterized by effort and striving and the concomitant mental states of anxiety and stress, but is fundamentally passive.

Dr Green maintains that biofeedback techniques have an immense advantage over other mind training systems in that the immediate feedback of information enables the process to be greatly speeded up. It takes a long time for someone practising yogic disciplines to 'develop inside-the-skin awareness', but biofeedback enables people to change a number of physiological variables at the same time and to develop the ability to do so in a remarkably short time. When a person has learned to control his internal states with the help of biofeedback instruments, he is encouraged to continue his self-regulation training without the instruments and is generally able to do so.

Dr Green showed film of experiments conducted in his psychophysiology laboratory with two adepts of mind-body control – an Indian yogi called Swami Rama and a 'Western Sufi' from Holland called Jack Schwarz. Swami Rama demonstrated control of the arteries in his wrist by simultaneously warming up one spot on the palm of his hand and cooling down another spot only two inches away until there was a difference of eleven degrees Fahrenheit between them. He then slowed down his heart beat from seventy beats a minute to fifty-two beats a minute, taking less than a minute to effect the change. Not content with this, he offered for the sake of the experiment to stop his heart beating completely for three or four minutes, but Dr Green said that an arrest of ten seconds would be enough to prove his point. In fact, Swami Rama stopped his heart pumping blood for seventeen seconds, putting it in the state that is known as 'atrial flutter', before a stop was called to the experiment. Jack Schwarz demonstrated pain control by showing no physiological pain responses when burning cigarettes were held against his forearm for as long as twenty-five seconds. He was also seen to drive a knitting needle through his biceps and to control the bleeding when it was removed. Two seconds after he said, 'Now it stops,' the bleeding stopped and shortly afterwards there was no sign of a wound. A significant fact reported by Dr Green was that both Swami Rama and Jack Schwarz were able to report correctly on the past, present and future mental, emotional and physical conditions of persons whom they did not know and had never seen. This fact, which is even more inexplicable in terms of prevailing scientific concepts than is mind-body self-regulation, would seem to substantiate the claim of another of the May lecturers, Dr E. Stanton Maxey, that mind is a 'field phenomenon'. Attempting to explain how the powers that he demonstrated worked, Swami Rama said, 'The physical body is an energy structure. What you see is only a small piece of the energy structure and the whole energy structure contains a lot of subtle parts which you can't see. The physical part is just the densest part of it. I want you to know that all of the body is in the mind, but not all of the mind is in the body. There is a large energy structure and the body is only the densest section of it, and every piece of the body, every cell, you can control, because it's all in the mind. There are ten energies connected with this, called "pranas", which a man can learn to control. And in addition to the ten pranas inside the skin there are numerous pranas outside the skin, some of which he can also learn to control.' Swami Rama modestly claimed to be able to control only a couple of the pranas outside the skin.

I shall return to the 'field of mind' theory that this quotation from Swami Rama, as reported by Dr Green, adumbrates. But before we move into the more speculative area, let us return to biofeedback and consider some of its implications. Apart from being an interesting demonstration of the fact that man can control physiological processes that are usually regarded as involuntary, what can biofeedback achieve and how does it work?

Dr Green offers a diagrammatic schema of the biofeedback process (Figure 9) which shows it as a 'cybernetic loop'.

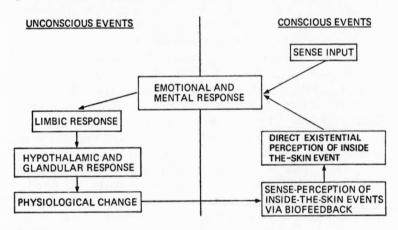

FIG. 9

In the diagram, a consciously perceived sense input leads to an emotional and/or mental response, which in turn produces a response in the limbic system, a neural complex which is sometimes known as the 'visceral brain' or the 'emotional brain'. The limbic system is connected by numerous neural pathways to the hypothalamic region of the brain, where the control centres of the autonomic nervous system are located. The hypothalamus is in turn connected the pituitary gland, which controls biochemical processes throughout the body. Thus physiological changes (for example in temperature, heart rate, etc.) are effected. Now the loop process moves across to the conscious area with a sense perception of inside-the-skin events through a reading of the information relayed by means of the biofeedback instruments. This results in a direct existential perception of the inside-the-skin event, which in turn leads back to complete the loop with an emotional and/or mental response to the inside-the-skin perception.

The question arises: where does volition enter into this process? Clearly, it does not enter into the neuro-biochemical events on the left of the diagram and accordingly it cannot be defined in such terms. A behaviouristic science cannot account for it. Yet it is seen to work, in the 'conscious events' area of the loop process, through the volitional use that the biofeedback subject makes of the inside-the-skin information. It has to be posited, Dr Green suggests, as a 'metaforce', a force that operates upon the physiological system but is not contained in it. Behaviourists may be sceptical of such a hypothesis, but anyone acquainted with modern subatomic physics, with its 'neutrinos' and 'quarks', will not find repugnant the hypothesis of a force which, though it cannot be located or defined in terms of prevailing concepts, is nevertheless seen to work. The necessity to posit volition as a 'metaforce', independent of neurochemical bodily processes, will be seen to lend further support to the idea that mind and consciousness are field phenomena.

Biofeedback research has practical as well as theoretical implications. Its techniques have been used in therapy with notable success. Migraine sufferers have learned to alleviate their condition by practising temperature control, which involves control of the vascular system and of the flow of blood through the brain. People suffering from tension headaches have gained relief from muscle tension feedback. Swami Rama deliberately induced his 'atrial flutter', but people prone to the condition have learned to control it with the help of a biofeedback meter connected to an electrocardiograph. Epileptics, too, have benefited from biofeedback training, by learning to produce alpha brain rhythms. Even alcoholics and drug addicts have been helped, though there is no physiological information relevant to their conditon that can be fed back to them by means of the biofeedback instruments. In such cases it seems to have been sufficient for a therapeutic effect for the addict to learn through biofeedback training that he was not necessarily a slave to uncontrollable compulsions but could in fact learn to master certain of his physiological processes. The resultant change in the subject's self-image itself had a therapeutic effect.

These are specific therapeutic applications of biofeedback. A further development of Dr. Green's work has been an exploration of those states of consciousness in which the imagination functions most creatively. Creativity is associated with the production of the low frequency brain rhythms known as alpha and theta waves (theta waves being of the lower frequency and associated with states of deep reverie and intuition). Dr Green has posed the question 'Can creativity be learned?' and has developed means of training suitable subjects in the production of alpha and theta waves. By adding a fourth and fifth bar to the feedback panel he has made it possible for his subjects to monitor their success in producing alpha and theta waves and to develop the ability to do so. He reports a considerable degree of success in his experiments to date.

Theta brain rhythms are often accompanied by 'hypnagogic' imagery – imagery that comes suddenly into the mind from an unconscious source and that is akin to the 'flashes' of vision or insight that poets and intuitive scientists experience. Dr Green's research subjects report a greatly increased incidence of hypnagogic imagery, and also a tendency to experience imagery of a kind that a Jungian psychologist would call 'archetypal' and would regard as issuing from the 'collective unconscious'. They further report an ability to recall past experiences in minute detail and with extraordinary vividness, a vividness more like really reliving the experiences rather than dreaming about them. Literary readers will be reminded of James Joyce's 'epiphanies' and of Proust's total recall of the past triggered by the taste of a madeleine biscuit. But perhaps the most important result of Dr Green's research into creativity is one that he professes not to have anticipated: a high frequency of integrative experiences. Many of his subjects reported an enhanced sense of personal identity and purpose, greater confidence and capacity for concentration, a sustained sense of elation, increased perceptiveness, better relations with others and a more developed sense of responsibility. Anyone acquainted with Abraham Maslow's *Toward a Psychology of Being* will not find these results surprising. Maslow has clearly shown that what he calls 'peak experiences' (visionary or integrative experiences) are 'acute identity experiences' and result in improvements in the psychological, emotional and social lives of individuals similar to those that Dr Green's biofeedback subjects have reported. The efficacy of biofeedback training in certain kinds of therapy has been proved, but the most significant aspect of Dr Green's research may ultimately prove to be in this area of alpha-theta training and the fostering of creativity. The use of psychedelic drugs, hypnotism in its various forms (including the collective hypnotism of the religious ritual), sensory deprivation or mortification of the flesh to induce visionary or integrative experiences may ultimately be seen to be crude means of approach in comparison with a method that requires only will, patience and the assistance, for monitoring purposes, of electronic technology.

That man can 'will' changes in his internal states may be taken as proved by Dr Green's carefully controlled researches. Volition undoubtedly works; but how it works is a question to which, in the present state of our knowledge, only a conjectural and not an empirical answer can be given. As we have seen, Dr Green could find no place for it in neurochemical terms in his 'cybernetic loop' and had to posit it as a 'metaforce'. The concept of a 'metaforce' may be illustrated by the example of a thermostatically controlled temperature system. Such a system cannot deviate from its programmed behaviour. But a human hand can alter the programme, can set the thermostat at a higher or lower level. The human hand in relation to the thermostatically controlled system functions as a metaforce. Volition is analogous. It is a force from outside the physiological system that can determine how the system operates. The analogy may be pursued further. The hand that controls the thermostat has an owner, and the owner's actions are purposeful, they are not isolated and arbitrary but have a place in the context of his life; they are actions related to life-support or life-enhancement needs, needs which may be primary and instinctual or conscious and deliberately pursued. Similarly, volition is a force that does not exist on its own but relates back to a complex of ideas, assumptions and purposes held by an individual. And some of these ideas and purposes may be unconscious or transpersonal, may belong to areas where the life-system of that individual meets and coincides with other life-systems of which his is a part – such as that of his community, his culture, or at a further remove that of Nature or the cosmos. The phenomenon of volition is not necessarily a case of the individual will pursuing a conscious end, but is more plausibly imaged as a part receiving information and direction from the whole.

This brings us back to the idea of volition as a 'field phenomenon'. 'Thought', said Dr Stanton Maxey in one of the May Lectures, 'is a form of energy; it has universal "field" properties which both affect and are affected by intertwining gravity, sound, light, magnetic, electrostatic, life, and other thought fields.' We shall see later that such a conception is necessary to explain some of the stranger phenomena of parapsychology. That a man can voluntarily control internal states and processes in himself, which traditional psychology has regarded as involuntary, is an idea not too far removed from by now widely accepted principles of psychosomatics. But that he can know, diagnose and control such states in others, that other forms of life, even plants, can be attuned to his mental processes, that he can mentally influence the behaviour of material things, are propositions that in terms of prevailing ideas about man and Nature are literally nonsensical. If these propositions are true they can only be explained in terms of a 'field theory of mind' such as Dr Green and Dr Maxey have hypothesized. In the next section I shall examine some of the strange evidence that not only supports such a theory, but makes it indispensable.

On Cognition

Traditional philosophy presents a picture of a wealth of human ingenuity squandered on a paucity of factual evidence. And traditional science has accumulated a wealth of data but has lacked the temerity to set it in a conceptual framework. Though both their professions have as their aim the pursuit of truth, philosophers and scientists have tended to eschew each other's areas of specialization. It has been regarded as a 'professional' virtue of the philosopher to be sceptical, and of the scientist to be specific. Their respective disciplines have declared it 'unphilosophical' to admit as truth any facts that fail to satisfy the most stringent principles of verification, and as 'unscientific' any attempt to generalize or hypothesize on the findings of specific research. The result has been that philosophers have had too little to philosophize about, and scientists have been too incurious, sometimes even too irresponsible, about the implications of their work. By their own default they have yielded the ground between their two disciplines to the non-specialist, the amateur, whom they both, from their professional standpoints, tend to disparage.

Take, for instance, the question of cognition. Listening to one of the May lecturers, Cleve Backster, on the topic 'Do Plants Think?', I could not help wondering what Descartes, Berkeley, Locke or Russell would have made of it all. Worried as they were by the questions of the reality of the external world, the existence of other minds, the reliability of sense-data, the possibility of asserting with confidence anything except the *cogito,* and the statement 'I think', what would they have made of Cleve Backster's evidence that cognition is not exclusively a faculty of the introspecting self, nor even generally of human minds, but exists even in plants and eggs? The question is rhetorical. Of course, traditional empiricism would not admit Mr Backster's evidence as satisfying its demanding principles of verification. So much the worse for traditional empiricism! The philosophical, inquiring mind in man is not satisfied with reductionist philosophies; when new knowledge, scientifically verified, comes to light, the inquiring mind seeks an integrative philosophy to contain it. It is such research as Cleve Backster's that has led to the development in recent years of 'systems philosophy'. Though none of the May lecturers mentioned 'systems philosophy' as such, many of the researches reported on and the hypotheses offered in the course of the lectures endorse and parallel the work of Ervin Laszlo, Ludwig van Bertalanffy and other 'systems' philosophers. I shall have more to say about these correspondences later. Now let us take a look at the evidence for the existence of cognition, or 'primary perception' as Cleve Backster calls it, in plants and rudimentary animal organisms.

Two of the May lecturers had contributions to make on this topic – Cleve Backster, who is Director of the American Polygraph Association, and Dr Marcel Vogel, who is Senior Chemist with I.B.M. in San Jose, California. Dr Vogel quoted Charles Darwin and Dr Jagadis Chandra Bose as early researchers who had pointed out correspondences between the nervous systems and life-forms of plants and of humans. He offered as the considered conclusion of his own experience of 'Interpersonal Communication Between Man and Plant' (the title of his talk) this formulation: 'There is intelligence in every living cell that is on this planet. It is called cellular consciousness. It is that which maintains the form of that cell.' He further claimed that there is 'intercellular communication', and implied that this cannot be explained in biochemical terms or in terms of neuron activity in the brain because it takes place between cells belonging to different living organisms.

Dr Vogel had little concrete scientific evidence to offer in support of his theories, but his sincerity, his enthusiasm and his conviction were both engaging and impressive. And the lack of hard evidence in his lecture was amply compensated for by the wealth of it in Cleve Backster's. Mr Backster prefaced his report on his researches with some cautionary remarks for the credulous. 'An observation', he said, 'is not an experiment.' He had made hundreds of observations, but had only published one experiment; 'and even a series of experiments', he said, 'doesn't constitute a proof.' He then proceeded to talk about his work in a manner that suggested that even if he was not claiming that it proved anything he certainly thought that it challenged scientists and philosophers to take notice and to reassess their positions in the light of it.

Mr Backster gave an account of his 'first encounter with

plants so far as a testing situation was concerned'. This was in February 1966. He was engaged on some conventional polygraph research when, during a coffee break, he idly watered a plant in the laboratory and it occurred to him that it would be interesting to find out how long it took the water to get from the roots into the leaves. So he attached two steel electrodes to one of the plant's leaves, and when he read the polygraph chart he recognized on it a 'people-like reaction curve'. He checked the instruments for possible faults in the wiring, and in the course of doing so an image of fire entered his mind. He then found that the chart reading for that moment when he entered the image of fire showed 'a wild state of agitation' in the plant. He went into a neighbouring office, fetched a box of matches from a drawer, focused his thoughts on an intention to burn the plant, and again got a 'wild reading' from the chart. When he removed the threat and put away the matches, the signs of agitation disappeared. So excited was he by all this that he felt like rushing out into Times Square and declaring to the world, 'A plant just read my mind,' and only the thought of jeopardizing his reputation as a serious scientist restrained him.

Cleve Backster then invited various members of the scientific community to offer explanations for the phenomenon. He asked a botanist, a biologist, a zoologist, a chemist, a psychologist, and even – he added wryly – a psychiatrist! But no one could suggest an explanation, so he proposed that they should co-operate on a controlled experiment.

The experiment was published in the winter 1968 issue of the *International Journal of Parapsychology* under the title 'Evidence of a Primary Perception in Plant Life'. Mr Backster wrote in the conclusion of his paper:

> The significance of the experiment results provides evidence of the existence of a yet undefined primary perception in plant life, indicates that animal life termination can serve as a remotely located stimulus to demonstrate this capability, and illustrates that this facility in plants can be independent of human involvement . . .
> Based upon Backster Research Foundation observa-

tions, the author hypothesises that this perception facility may be part of a primary sensory system capable of functioning at cell level. This is further suggested by observation of its apparent presence in plant and animal tissue separated from an organism (including human), and maintained *in vitro* where the specialized senses are not present ...

Research approaches now seem practical in areas which have been elusive in the past regarding compliance with the strict standards required by scientific methodology. Opportunities could well exist for productive investigation of diverse psychological phenomena, including the study of group interaction and the possibility of allowing deeper insight into cellular 'blueprints,' as related to individual cell functions within the developing organism. New dimensions may be found in genetics and in life-matter interrelationship. On the basis of preliminary exploration, the author considers productive research to be possible in all of these, as well as in other areas ...

The Backster Research Foundation subsequently devoted hundreds of hours to the observation of plants, often in circumstances where no attempt was made to influence their behaviour. Some extraordinary behavioural patterns emerged. It appeared that plants have a sense of territory. They would show sensitivity to events occurring in other rooms in the laboratory area, but show no reaction at all to events in other rooms in the building that were nearer to them but unconnected with the activities of the laboratory. They also seemed to be responsive to the emotional experiences of the people looking after them and would show a stress reaction to anxiety states in such people even though they were twenty or thirty miles away. Using stop-watches and electroencephalograph readings, Backster conducted some careful experiments on this phenomenon at such distances and obtained chart readings showing agitation that synchronized with the moment of stress or anxiety experienced by the absent member of the research team. He obtained the same result in an experiment that he described as 'less careful' in that it involved a possible margin of error in synchronization, when he monitored the reaction of a laboratory plant while a member of his team was on a journey, taking the touch-down time of her plane at an airport seven hundred miles away as the moment when she might be expected to experience stress and anxiety.

The research produced amusing moments as well as exciting and surprising ones. On one occasion a woman scientist, a plant physiologist, visited the laboratory. She was working on methods of forcing and speeding up plant growth in order to increase crop yield. Backster connected electrodes to six laboratory plants, but not one of them showed a reaction to her and he had to resort to showing her records of chart readings to demonstrate his research. But when she left, every one of the plants jumped for joy!

Another incident took place when Backster was demonstrating plant reactions monitored through a polygraph to a group of graduate students at Yale University. They brought a spider into the laboratory, put it on a table, and one student frustrated the spider's efforts to get away by enclosing it with his hands. When he removed his hands, the spider remained still for some seconds, then began to move rapidly. At the moment when it began to move the polygraph showed a wild reaction. This happened several times. They then decided to let the spider go down the carpeted staircase leading to the floor below and to try to find it by following the polygraph readings. So one student was on his hands and knees searching the staircase, while another was calling to him from above, telling him how close he was by following the spider's stress reactions transmitted by the plant to the polygraph.

This anecdote illustrates another curious observation that the Backster Research Foundation made about plants: that they seem to be responsive to stress or pain experienced by other living things within their environment. They conducted an experiment which involved dropping live shrimps into boiling water while a plant was wired to a polygraph at the other end of the laboratory. To obviate the possibility of interference by the consciousness of the people present, the experiment was completely automated. The chart reading showed a strong reaction from the plant on most occasions when a shrimp was dropped into the boiling water, but on other occasions there was no reaction at all. Further investigation revealed that the plant was not reacting to shrimps' that were dead or dying, but only to the healthy ones. Fortunately, there is no Society for the Prevention of Cruelty to Shrimps. Anyway, in his recent research, Backster has moved on from using 'animal life termination' as the remote stimulus (see the first paragraph quoted on page 203) to using a positive stimulus based on 'nutrient reward'. He has also moved on from plants to bacteria cultures, chicken eggs, human sperm and blood, working on the hypothesis that there is 'a primary sensory system ... functioning at cell level'. A typical experiment of this type was one in which nutrient was automatically injected into a bacteria culture in one incubator while electroencephalograph readings were recorded from a second incubator remotely located in the same laboratory environment. Backster describes the results of initial research of this type as 'extremely encouraging'.

Though Cleve Backster entitled his talk 'Do Plants Think?', the question that he is really concerned with goes much further than this title suggests. It might be formulated as: does such a thing as intercellular communication exist? An experiment conducted in Russia and reported by Marcel Vogel in his talk throws more light on this question. Two identical tissue cells from a human body were placed in dishes made of quartz. One dish was put on top of the other. The cells in the top dish were then poisoned with strychnine, and when they died the cells in the lower dish died too. However, when pyrex dishes were substituted for the quartz dishes, the cells in the lower dish were not affected. The difference between pyrex and quartz is that the former does not pass short-wave electrical impulses. The experiment would seem to afford evidence for the field theory of consciousness that Dr Green and Dr Maxey independently put forward in their contributions to the May Lectures.

We move now from the realm of fact and exploration into that of conjecture. History has seen many and various paradigms of man, mind and Nature triumph, flourish awhile and then be superseded. The contentions of the philosophical factions are bewildering enough to make any man, except one in whom knowledge is a hunger and intellect a passion, take refuge in relativism or in the aphilosophical attitude expressed in Bertrand Russell's sally: 'What is mind? It doesn't matter. What is matter? Never mind.' And what indeed does it matter whether you see man as an aggregation of 'humours' or adopt a mechanistic, a vitalistic or a behaviouristic view? It matters only, I suppose, to those who obstinately believe that one day the truth will out. Such believers may take encouragement from the fact that the above-mentioned paradigms were directly related to and derived from the state of scientific knowledge in their day, and that in recent years, with the aid of advanced technology, science has gained access to areas of knowledge that were previously impenetrable. It would be folly to claim that any final truth has emerged or is emerging from modern investigations in the fields of molecular biology, psychophysiology and paranormal psychology, but it is undeniable that new facts have emerged and are emerging all the time, and that these new facts will constitute the basis for a new paradigm of man, mind and Nature. The 'field theory' that several of the May lecturers postulated or asserted would appear to be a sketch for a new paradigm.

Dr Marcel Vogel put it most boldly: 'We generate a field at the cellular level. We generate composite fields at the mental level, and we generate the most potent force in the world at the conscious level. I have seen physical objects moved by the conscious power of the mind.'

Parapsychology deals with experiences and behaviour that defy known physical laws. Conventional science assumes that man relates to his environment through his sensory and his motor systems. Parapsychology takes as its point of departure the fact that human beings have experiences that cannot be explained in terms of sensory or motor functions. Electronic technology has extended the range of what cannot be so explained beyond the subjective experiences of human beings to the behaviour of other life-forms. Parapsychology thus finds itself forced to pursue its researches into the territory of other scientists – of biologists, physicists, botanists, chemists, physiologists. Its basic problem is that the phenomena it deals with are not physical, are not related to any localized body organs of substances that can be observed or analyzed. Only the effects can be observed, and the causes remain a matter of conjecture. A plausible conjecture would seem to be that if the effective causes or paranormal experiences and behaviour have no specific location, they may have a general extension; or, to put it another way, if they are not material, they may be a property of matter. Thus we come to 'field theory'.

The environment of every living organism includes fields of force: gravity, magnetics, electrostatics, sound and light. Living organisms do not only exist in an environment constituted by these force fields. They also contain them, use them, depend on them. The word 'environment' is misleading. We are speaking about forces that permeate life rather than surround it. Cosmic rays are all the time passing through each one of us. Photosynthesis, the process by which light energy is converted to proteins by plants, is the basis for animal and human physical existence. Radio energy in the microwave range affects chromosomes and genes in human beings, and sound waves of very low frequency (three to five cycles per second) can kill a man. The air we breathe contains ions, clusters of molecules with positive or negative charges. Positive ion atmospheres can cause respiratory troubles, headaches, depressions and even heart attacks, whereas negative ion atmospheres can produce a forty per cent increase in human reaction times; and the ionic change in the atmosphere is affected by magnetic field forces. These examples (cited by Dr Stanton Maxey in his lecture 'Man, Mind, Matter and Fields') demonstrate that all living organisms participate in a complex interplay of fields and forces and in a constant process of energy exchange. Every living cell is charged with energy and is 'a tiny electric battery generating its own current by chemical action' (Dr George Crile, quoted by Dr Maxey). This much is known and scientifically attested. The question then is: can we assume, on the basis of this body of knowledge, that cognition, consciousness and thought are also 'field phenomena'? Dr Maxey, Dr Vogel, Dr Green and Cleve Backster all believe that we can. Nevertheless, the assumption remains an argument by analogy, and arguments by analogy are notably

fallible. This is not to say that we should not pursue such
arguments or make such assumptions. Philosophical
paradigms are not just clusters of scientifically attested facts;
they are intellectual structures based upon a body of facts
that are seen or made to form a coherent picture, and often
the argument by analogy is used to make the facts cohere. A
paradigm dies a natural death when a body of new facts
which it cannot contain or explain come to light or gradually
accumulate; and a new paradigm is born when somebody
puts forward a principle or schema that affords a coherent
picture of the new body of knowledge and at the same time
subsumes the old. It can be said of the 'field theory' of
volition and cognition that it succeeds in doing this. I doubt
that there is any other theory that could be put forward at
the present time that could better explain the facts brought
to light by Elmer Green and Cleve Backster in their careful
and unimpeachably scientific researches into the life functions of volition and cognition.

'Field theory', however, should be seen in a broad context as
a contribution to systems philosophy. Traditional philosophy
has been stuck with the problem of the subjectivity of
knowledge. There is no way out of this problem so long as we
take human mind events (perceptions, sensations, memories,
intuitions, judgments, etc.) as our only means of gaining
knowledge of the world. We cannot know how mind events
relate to the physical events that we suppose to be their
causes. A neutral transfer or chemical discharge in a brain
cell is of a different order of reality from greenness, hardness,
extension, existence, or any other quality we may, as 'naive
realists', attribute to things in that objective world. It follows
that we cannot know for certain that there is an objective
world. Traditional philosophy, taking human mind events as
the only knowable data, ends up with an insuperable
dualism of the mental and physical, the subjective and
objective worlds. Systems philosophy does not get bogged
down in the dilemma of dualism because it does not base
itself on anthropomorphic categories. It takes organization as
its criterion of reality and focuses attention on structures and
functions. Its conceptual model of the world envisages it as
a complex of interconnected systems. It does not regard man

as set apart from the world, a detached observer perplexed about the relevance of his observations, but it sees him as a functioning system within the complex of systems that make up the world. Furthermore, as it does not regard man and Nature as belonging to different orders of reality, systems philosophy does not attribute exclusive properties or functions either to man or to Nature. The idea of mind events occurring in Nature at any point between the single cell and the macrocosm does not violate the fundamental principles of systems philosophy. In fact, evidence of the occurrence of such events in Nature lends support to these fundamental principles. Though I would not presume to say that Dr Green, Dr Maxey and Cleve Backster need systems philosophy, I think it is true to say that systems philosophy needs the empirical evidence that the researches of these men and others have brought to light

On Uncanny Powers

Anybody who writes, reads or thinks about parapsychological phenomena has at some stage to confront the problem of his own credulity threshold. He is going to be asked to believe some quite incredible things, so he needs to be clear at least about two things: how exacting are his own standards of proof; and to what extent is his intellectual assent influenced by emotional or temperamental factors? Man needs beliefs – and the bored, the underprivileged, the unqualified, the disaffected, the social misfits and the rebels are all strongly predisposed to believe in anything that mocks orthodox science or religion and its custodians. The support of such people can only do damage to parapsychology as a science and retard its progress. It is a young science and it often deals with subjects about which a great deal of misinformation and superstition has accumulated, and anyone concerned with it in any way must realize that herein lie dangers. Its methods and its proofs need to be rigorous, controlled and objective.

The cause of parapsychology as a science, as a quest for knowledge, is surely not helped by allegations of conspiracy either by its critics or its supporters. Yet the literature of the subject abounds with such allegations. It is claimed on the one hand that orthodox science deliberately suppresses and ignores facts that it cannot explain in its own terms, and on the other hand that a group of maverick deserters from the scientific disciplines are bent on undermining the foundations of science itself and are not above using fraud to attain their ends. Though an element of truth may be conceded to both these claims – there are obstinate, entrenched conservatives and unprincipled opportunists in most professions – such allegations are really quite negative and unprofitable.

We can, I think, say with some confidence that man has not yet attained through his sciences a complete knowledge of himself and his environment; that the concepts and methods of science differ from culture to culture; that myth, religion and even superstition testify to the fact that there are areas of perennial human experience and concern that have not been systematically mapped and demystified; and that it is at least possible that inherent in its conceptual and methodological framework there are limits to what any science can know and do. If so much is admitted, there can be no rational objection to the subject matter of parapsychology. A man cannot be called a freak, a renegade or a fool for investigating, for example, clairvoyance, spiritualism, or psychic healing. Such criticism, which many parapsychological investigators will testify is still not uncommon, is both impertinent and arrogant.

Critical scrutiny of the methods employed in parapsychological research, however, is not only legitimate but also essential for the health and reputation of the science. New areas of research require new methods of investigation, and the chief function of the scientist is to devise such methods to test his hypotheses. The terms 'occult' and 'scientific' do not designate clearly demarcated areas of knowledge. Scientific method has over the centuries conquered areas of knowledge that were once occult in the sense of 'hidden'. I have already reported how the scientific method has fathomed secrets of human volition and creativity and of 'primary perception' in plant and animal life, subjects that not long ago would have been considered inaccessible to investigation and therefore occult. And there is a great deal of conscientious research and experiment being done today that will bring many phenomena and experiences at present considered occult into the light of scientific knowledge.

But 'occult' does not only mean 'hidden', it also means 'supernatural' or 'magical'. There are areas that scientific method cannot gain access to, and it is with regard to these areas that we all have to examine and define our own credulity threshold. Anyone with an inquiring, open mind will respond to the invitation, 'See, and you will believe'. There is no problem. We examine the evidence, judge the manner in which it was obtained, and reach our own conclusion. But what do we do when the invitation is, 'Believe, and you will see'?

I am now going to report on the contributions to the May Lectures made by two men who, in effect, issued such an invitation. They presented evidence to support their claims, but they did not claim that the evidence was rigorously scientific. They were both men with high academic qualifications and reputations, and with backgrounds of years of work in practical sciences. Lyall Watson, whose book *Supernature* has had a great success in England this year, reported on his observations of psychic surgery in the Philippines. And Andrija Puharich, writer of the authorized biography of Uri Geller, talked about his research work with the famous Israeli psychic.

Lyall Watson entitled his lecture, 'Is Primitive Medicine Really Primtive?'. And he answered the question with an emphatic negative, giving an account, supported by film, of the work of 'psychic surgeons' that he had witnessed in Manila.

He prefaced his report with anecdotes about other experiences he had had of uncanny psychic powers and with some remarks on the limitations of Western medical science. His personal turning point had come when, after ten years of academic training in natural science, he had, on a visit to India, seen a street-corner fakir in Madras reply to a mocking American tourist, a professed Christian, by causing a bleeding stigmata to appear in the palms of her hands. Later he had seen the same man's ten-year-old son 'drink' water from his hands by sucking it up through the pores of his skin.

These incidents, impossible and unscientific as they were, had caused him to question the validity of his own training and fundamental beliefs about science and medicine, and particularly to question 'the dogmatic certainty that we all unfortunately share in the validity of our particular perceptions, in our specific interpretations of reality, in judgments that we have learned to make in common and accept as exclusive fact.' His experiences made him realize that 'there are other realities, all real, and ours is only one of the possible descriptions of how things really are.' Most of our knowledge, what we call scientific knowledge included, is a matter of blind faith. We believe things because they have been proved by other people by scientific method. That method is based on observation, but observation of a particular kind of reality. It develops a theory to account for that reality and ends with an experimental proof of the theory. But no one can personally verify by experiment more than a fraction of what he believes to be true. Most of us believe, for example, in the existence of the electron, but our belief is not based on personal observation but on faith in the scientific process and in the testimony of professional physicists. What if a metaphysician tells us that an electron is a departed soul? We will probably reject his interpretation and accept the physicist's, not because we know the latter to be truer but because we believe it to be more authoritative, because we have a cultural and intellectual bias in favour of the physicist's interpretation of the truth. We should examine this bias, Watson argues. If we do so, we will realize that we have a restrictive intellectual approach to information which is governed by our senses, and particularly by the sense of sight. We subordinate all our other senses, intuitive as well as physical, to the sense of sight, and base our ideas of what is real and true on its sole testimony. And we continue to do this even though it is well established by now that perception is, as phenomenologists say, 'intentional' – that we see what we expect to see and often just do not register what is unexpected, unusual or unfamiliar. How can we get out of our cultural straitjacket, how can we learn to bring all our senses and faculties to bear upon our quest for knowledge? One way, Watson suggests, is to go with an open mind and observe other cultures; to directly experience their methods and the beliefs and attitudes that inform them.

So he went to the Philippines. Believing that Western attitudes to health and healing are restricted and impoverished by prevailing scientific ideas and socio-cultural factors, Watson went to observe at first hand the work of the famous psychic healers of Manila.

The cultural background of these people is an amalgam. It is aboriginal overlaid by Catholic Christianity as a result of four centuries of Spanish occupation and, more recently, by American influence. The latter has introduced modern Western allopathic medicine, which the Philippinos avail themselves of for a class of ailment that Watson calls 'natural' (burns, fractures, etc.). But for other types of ailment they go to a medicine man or psychic healer. Watson distinguishes two other types of ailment – the 'dull' (long-lasting illnesses that are hard to cure, like cancer) and the 'sharp' (seizures, epilepsy, heart attacks), and suggests that these might be better treated by a method that combines ritual, magic and medicine than by the Western method of hospitalization and specialist treatment. The 'primitive' method has the advantage that it socializes disease and its cure (operations are done in informal situations with spectators around), and reinforces the sufferer's sense of being a part of the society and of life rather than one of its victims. We may be sceptical of miracle cures, but would anyone be so intransigent and narrow-minded as to deny that social factors, the attitudes and behaviour of others – of family, friends, witnesses – might play a part in the healing situation?

The psychic healers of Manila have their individual techniques and specializations, but there are certain characteristics that they have in common. They all precede their work with some kind of prayer or ritual, they all work in communal situations – with perhaps forty or fifty people assembled in a small place, watching, participating, waiting their turn – and they all operate in a state of detachment, often in a trance-like state. Many operations involve 'removing' some alien object from the body. There is a woman healer who specializes in this. Watson has observed her closely hundreds of times and has seen her 'remove' a whole corncob, a bunch of leaves, a plastic bag, a rusty nail, a piece of glass and numerous other objects. He is convinced that this is not merely clever conjuring. The objects simply appear on the body surface in a split second. Another healer takes objects that look like coffee beans out of people's eyes. A film showed this and there was no possibility that the healer had palmed the object because it appeared from under the eyelid when his hand was nowhere near. Watson believes that the only explanation of this phenomenon is that the objects materialize on the body surface. He witnessed another extraordinary case of materialization when a healer claimed to be able to cure a friend of his who was in Africa at the time. He rolled a piece of paper into the shape of a trumpet, put it to his mouth and drew into it a thick liquid that looked and smelled foul. He did this several times, filled a pot with at least two pints of the liquid, and then announced that Watson's friend was cured.

Another common practice among the healers is to give 'injections', or make incisions in the skin with a finger movement made at a distance of one or two feet from the body. Watson reports that he personally experienced this. He put a plastic sheet across his chest. The healer pointed at his chest, moved his finger and a cut appeared on his chest though the plastic was not marked.

The most common and most dramatic type of operation performed involves manual manipulation on the body surface. Watson showed a film in which a German woman was operated on for a liver complaint by the best-known of the Philippine healers, Tony Agpao. Wearing only light trousers and a shirt with the sleeves rolled up, Agpao exposed his open hands to the camera to show that there was nothing hidden, then proceeded to knead the flesh with his hands. Blood soon appeared, then after further manipulation a section of tissue appeared on the body and was removed. It looked as if the woman's body had been opened and a deep internal operation performed, but when Agpao removed his hands and the blood was swabbed away there was no sign of an incision on the woman's skin. Her own doctor gave an account of her medical history over twenty years and vouched for the fact that after this operation her condition was greatly improved.

Having witnessed many such operations, Watson is dubious whether the body is ever actually penetrated, but he is convinced that there is no deception involved in making blood and tissue appear on the body. He believes that they are materializations. He has examined tumours obtained in this way. They are not always human, but he does not think that this fact invalidates the treatment or proves that there is fraud. The fact remains that patients treated by psychic surgery are very often fully cured.

Before he met or heard of Uri Geller, Andrija Puharich had also done research into psychic surgery. The subject of his study was the Brazilian healer, Arigo. A film of Arigo at work showed him roughly thrusting a small sharp knife into a patient's eye socket, moving it about and scraping the cornea. The patient showed no sign of pain. Puharich reported the Arigo effected many cures of leukaemia with prescriptions that were nothing more than combinations of common proprietary drugs, and that when the same combination was prescribed by somebody else it had no effect. He also reported that he had witnessed many operations performed by Arigo. He had seen him cut a person's stomach open, remove a diseased section of the large intestine and join the severed ends of the intestine simply by holding them together for a short time – and all this without using an anaesthetic or sterilized instruments. Arigo performed hundreds of operations like this, and in no case were any post-operative complications reported – no infection, no signs of shock. What kind of energy, Puharich asks, is used to accomplish these feats that baffle medical science?

His work with Arigo was halted by the healer's sudden death in a motor accident. But then he heard of Uri Geller, and his lifelong interest in parapsychological research took him to Israel. He soon became a close friend of Geller's, has recently written and published his biography, and is now devoting all his time and efforts to the task of scientifically validating Geller's psychic powers and informing the world of their staggering implications.

The scientific validation done to date has been sufficiently thorough and well documented to convince any sceptic that Geller does possess uncanny powers. Tests conducted at the Stanford Research Institute in California under strictly controlled conditions have established that Geller is capable of telepathy, clairvoyance, precognition and psychokinesis; that he can exercise control both over living systems and inanimate objects, making them disappear and reappear in another place; and that he can produce numerous other effects which modern science cannot begin to explain.

Dr Puharich described some of the tests. Geller's demonstrations usually begin with simple telepathy – guessing numbers, words or names written down by one of the observers. The Stanford researchers devised a test in which the 'target' material was a design made by a computer as a result of a series of numbers being punched out at random on a keyboard. The shape of the design was therefore unknown to any of the researchers, and it remained stored in the computer until Geller, alone in another room, had drawn his design. When the two shapes were compared they were identical.

In a test of clairvoyance, Geller has repeatedly been able to name correctly the upper face of a dice cast in a locked steel box. He has even been able to predict which face would be uppermost before the box was shaken.

He has a proven ability to affect scientific instruments, weighing balances, gauss meters, oscillators, etc. In one test, an object was placed on an electronic balance under a bell jar and Geller was able to effect changes in its mass, making it become heavier or lighter at will. He has also frequently demonstrated an ability to erase recording from video-tape by concentrated mental efforts.

His demonstrations of his control over living systems can be amusing or alarming. To see a plant held in the hand suddenly burst into flower within seconds or a four-inch bean sprout retract into the bean would delight any child; but to see a pet cat suddenly vanish from in front of his eyes would be a frightening experience, even though it did reappear in another place shortly afterwards. Puharich reports that Geller has produced this effect under controlled conditions using frogs, rats, mice and cats, and that none of the animals used in these tests have shown any biological, physiological or behavioural after-effects.

The power to make things materialize and dematerialize – which Lyall Watson also testified to having witnessed in the Philippines – is, of all the powers attributed to Geller, the most difficult to conceive. Yet it seems to be well attested by experienced scientific observers. In one test at Stanford a watch was put into a steel box, the box was sealed and one of the scientists actually sat upon it throughout the test. Geller was able to make the watch dematerialize and fall from the ceiling on to a test platform in another part of the room. When the steel box was opened, it was found to be empty and the watch on the platform had the same serial number as the one that had been placed in the box.

It is not possible to give a complete catalogue of all the 'Geller effects' in the space of this article. The interested reader is referred to Andrija Puharich's book, *Uri*.[1] The question that arises if we dismiss the possibility of fraud, as I think we must in view of the fact that many reputable scientists have substantiated Geller's and Puharich's claims, is this: do the phenomena indicate that laws of Nature exist which man's science has not yet comprehended, or are they contrary to and quite outside all natural laws?

Andrija Puharich does not answer this question, but he has an explanation of the Geller phenomena. He believes that he and Geller have been chosen by extra-terrestrial beings to bear witness to their existence and their powers, and to prepare mankind for a direct confrontation with these beings at some unspecified future date when they will make mass landings on earth. He believes that all Uri Geller's effects are demonstrations of the advanced science and civilization of these beings, whose attitude to man and his civilzation is benevolent and concerned. He bases these beliefs on the fact that he has frequently had two-way communication with them by means of a tape-recorder. They record messages on tape; he and Geller monitor the recording as it is being made through headphones and ask questions; then he transcribes the tape and as soon as he has done so the cassette disappears from inside the machine. 'No tape record of such voice recordings has been allowed to exist,' Puharich says.

Lyall Watson also reported instances of scientific or technological proof being mysteriously frustrated. An Italian
doctor took a gall-stone supposedly removed from a patient
by psychic surgery, put it in a screw-top container in his
pocket and found it missing from the container when he got
back to Italy, where he had intended to compare it with
X-ray pictures of the patient's gall-stone. Such stories, of
course, only confirm the sceptics in their scepticism, and one
may indeed wonder why, if Puharich's extra-terrestrial
beings want to let man know of their existence, they do not
allow the tapes to remain to substantiate Puharich's claims.
Though of course even if he did produce them and broadcast
them, there could be no proof that they were not frauds. Any
competent electronics technician can produce unearthly-
sounding synthesized speech. It really is difficult to imagine
any way in which Puharich could prove his contentions
either to the scientific community or to mankind at large. He
realizes this, in fact, and only asks that people keep open
minds and give some thought to the implications of his
revelations.

I imagine that this report will have tested the credulity
threshold of most readers. What do you do with ideas that
not only fall outside the scope of prevailing concepts of
reality but even invalidate them? What do you think of men
whose ability and sincerity is indisputable and who tell you
that your science, your philosophy and your quotidian
reality are partial and purblind? I personally have no
answers. I am convinced by other contributors to the May
Lectures that there is more to reality than meets the eye, and
more than our Western science and philosophy comprehend.
I am convinced that man has latent powers and enormous
potentials for further evolution. But as regards psychic surgery, materializations, dematerializations and beings from
outer space equipped with weird technologies I just do not
know; I can only say 'thank you' to Lyall Watson and
Andrija Puharich for contributing to that state of enligh-
tened mystification that may be the beginning of new
knowledge.

Notes

CHAPTER I *The End of Medicine and the Beginning of Health*

1. See, e.g. McCleery et al., *One Life - One Physician* (The Public Interest Press, 1971). This book compiles most of the medical care quality research prior to its publication.
2. See, e.g., Robert H. Brook, M.D., Sc.D., et al., 'Effectiveness of Non-Emergency Care via an Emergency Room', *Annals of Internal Medicine*, 77 (1973).
3. A. L. Cochrane, C.B.E., F.R.E.P., *Effectiveness and Efficiency* (The Nuffield Provincial Hospitals Trust, London, 1972).
4. See, e.g., Auster, Leveson and Sarachek, 'The Production of Health; An Exploratory Study', *Journal of Human Resources*, 4 (Fall 1969); and Victor Fuchs, 'The Contribution of Health Services to the American Economy', *Milbank Memorial Fund Quarterly*, 44 (October 1966) and *The Service Economy* (National Bureau of Economic Research, Washington, 1968).
5. See report of research in the *Rocky Mountain News*, September 6th, 1974.
6. See *Report of the Secretary's Commission on Medical Malpractice* (Department of Health, Education and Welfare, 1973).
7. Ivan Illich, *Medical Nemesis* (Calder and Boyars, London, 1974). See also Ivan Illich, 'Hygiene Nemesis', an unpublished paper (CIDOC, Cuernavaca, Mexico).
8. See, e.g., Ivan Illich, *Deschooling Society* (Calder and Boyars, London, 1971; Harper and Row, New York, 1970); *Tools for Conviviality* (Calder and Boyars, London, 1973; Harper and Row, New York, 1973); and *Energy and Equity* (Calder and Boyars, London, 1974; Harper and Row, New York, 1974).
9. See Dr Smith's essay in this volume, entitled 'Bioenergetics in Healing'.
10. See S. Krippner and D. Rubin, eds., *Galaxies of Life: The Human Aura in Acupuncture and Kirlian Photography* (Gordon and Breach, London, 1973).
11. See, e.g., Jerome Frank, *Persuasion and Healing* (Oxford University Press, London, 1961; Schocken Books, New York, 1961).
12. Andrew Weil, *The Natural Mind* (Jonathan Cape, London, 1973; Houghton Mifflin, New York, 1972), p. 173.

CHAPTER II *A New Paradigm?*

1. Leo Tolstoy, 'The Death of Ivan Illyich', trans. Margaret Webb, *Leo Tolstoi, Short Stories* (Progress Publishers, Moscow, n.d.), pp. 108-67.
2. Lawrence LeShan, *The Medium, the Mystic and the Physicist* (Viking Press, New York, 1974), p. 198.
3. Henry Marganau, 'E.S.P. in the Framework of Modern Science', *Science and E.S.P.*, J.R. Smythies, ed., (Routledge & Kegan Paul, London, 1967; Humanities Press, New York, 1967).
4. The axioms are based on Conant's work. See J.B. Conant, *Science and Common Sense* (Oxford University Press, London, 1951; Yale University Press, New Haven, 1951).
5. *Changing Images of Man*, Policy Research Report No. 4 (Center for the Study of Social Policy, Stanford Research Institute, Menlo Park, California, May 1974), pp. 82-3.
6. Barry Commoner, *The Closing Circle* (Jonathan Cape, London, 1972; Knopf, New York, 1971), p. 89.
7. The principle received a great boost in the physical sciences with the elaboration of the 'uncertainty' principle by Werner Heisenberg.
   For the behavioural sciences, see, e.g., Robert Rosenthal, 'Self-Fulfilling Prophecy', *Psychology Today* (New York, September 1968) and 'The Pygmalion Effect Lives', *Psychology Today* (New York, September 1973).
8. Jonas Salk, *The Survival of the Wisest* (Harper and Row, New York, 1973), p. 82.
9. Quoted in Arthur Koestler, *The Roots of Coincidence* (Hutchinson, London, 1972), p. 58.
10. Carlos Castaneda, *Tales of Power* (Simon & Schuster, New York, 1974). See also 'A Tale of Power', *Harper's* (New York, September 1974), p. 50.
11. Theodore Roszak, *Where the Wasteland Ends* (Doubleday, New York, 1972).
12. For a general view, see Edith Hamilton, *The Greek Way* (J.M. Dent & Sons, London, 1930; W.W. Norton, New York, 1930).
13. S. Leff and Vera Leff, *From Witchcraft to World Health* (Lawrence & Wishart, London, 1956; Macmillan, New York, 1957), p. 45.
14. Jerome Frank, *Persuasion and Healing* (Oxford University Press, London, 1961; Schocken Books, New York, 1961), p. 46.
15. Lord Ritchie-Calder, *Medicine and Man* (George Allen & Unwin, London, 1958; Signet Science Library, New York, 1958), p. 13.
16. Claude Levi-Strauss, quoted in Jerome Frank, op. cit.
17. William Irwin Thompson, 'Planetary Vistas', *Harper's* (New York, January 1971).
18. Andrew Weil, *The Natural Mind* (Jonathan Cape, London, 1973; Houghton Mifflin, New York, 1972), p.140.
19. Quoted in John Powles, 'On the Limitations of Modern Medicine', *Science, Medicine and Man*, 1 (London, 1973), p. 13.
20. Rudolf Virchow, *Cellular Pathology*, trans. Frank Chance (Ann Arbor, Michigan, 1858; reprinted by Edwards Brothers, 1940).

21. See Max von Pettenkofer, 'The Value of Health to a City', lectures quoted in *Bulletin of the History of Medicine*, 10 (1941), pp. 487-503.
22. René Dubos, *So Human an Animal* (Charles Scribners and Sons, New York, 1968), pp. 227-9.
23. A good brief account of their work can be found in Robert S. de Ropp, *The New Prometheans* (Jonathan Cape, London, 1972; Dell Publishing Co., New York, 1972).
24. See, e.g., Aaron Antonovsky, 'Breakdown; A Needed Armamentarium of Modern Medicine', *Social Science and Medicine*, 6 (London, 1972), pp. 537-44.
25. For a recent discussion of 'sick roles', see Siegler and Osmond, 'The Sick Role Revisited', *The Hastings Center Studies*, vol. 1, no. 3 (New York), p. 41.
26. Lawrence J. Henderson, *New England Journal of Medicine*, 270 (Massachusetts Medical Society, 1964), p. 449.
27. Kerr White, 'Health Care Arrangements in the United States: A.D. 1972', in 'Medical Care and Medical Cure', *The Milbank Memorial Fund Quarterly*, vol. 50, part 2, no. 4 (October 1972).
28. Robert Theobald, *Habit and Habitat* (Prentice-Hall, Inc., Englewood Cliffs, 1972), p. 1.
29. A.C. Crombie, 'The Future of Biology, The History of a Program', *Federal Proceedings*, 25 (1966), pp. 1448-53.
30. John Powles, op. cit., p. 15.

CHAPTER III *A New Medicine: Emerging Concepts and Research*

1. See, e.g., Barbara Brown, *New Mind, New Body* (Harper and Row, New York, 1974).
2. Lewis Thomas, M.D., 'I Am Less Intelligent Than My Liver', *New England Journal of Medicine*, 287 (Massachusetts Medical Society, 1972).
3. See e.g., R.K. Wallace and H. Benson, 'The Physiology of Meditation', *Psychology Today* (New York, April 1974).
4. Gay Gaer Luce, *Body Time: Physiological Rhythms and Social Issues* (Pantheon Books, New York, 1971).
5. See, e.g., research by Danish researchers in *New Scientist* (London, November 8th, 1973). There is also some research on specific wave functions. See, e.g., H. Kenig, 'Biological Effects of Extremely Low Frequency Electrical Phenomena in Atmosphere', *Journal of Interdisciplinary Cycle Research*, vol. 12, no. 3; and H.H. Heller, 'Cellular Effects of Microwave Radiation', *Symposium Proceedings* (Richmond, Virginia, September 1969).
6. Lyall Watson, *Supernature* (Hodder and Stoughton, London, 1973; Anchor Press, New York, 1973).
7. ibid.
8. John Ott, *Health and Light* (Devin-Adair, Co., Old Greenwich, Connecticut, 1973).
9. ibid., pp. 105-6.
10. S.R. Dean, M.D., 'The Psychic Mystique', a paper presented to the American Psychiatric Association, Dallas, Texas, May 2nd, 1972.

11. Albert Szent-Györgyi, *Bioelectronics, A Study in Cellular Regulation Defence and Cancer* (The Academic Press, New York, 1968).

12. Quoted in Peter Tompkins and Christopher Bird, *The Secret Life of Plants* (Allen Lane, London, 1974; Harper and Row, New York, 1973), p. 279.

13. Quoted in J. Bernstein, 'Profiles; The Secrets of the Old Ones', *New Yorker* (March 17th, 1973).

14. Quoted in Peter Tompkins and Christopher Bird, op. cit., p. 103.

15. Konrad Lorenz, *On Aggression* (Methuen, London, 1966; Harcourt, Brace and Wold Inc., New York, 1966).

16. John Bliebtrau, *The Parable of the Beast* (Victor Gollancz, London, 1968; Macmillan, New York, 1968).

17. Cleve Backster, 'Evidence of a Primary Perception in Plant Life', *International Journal of Parapsychology*, vol. 10, no. 4 (Winter 1968), p. 205.

18. Peter Tompkins and Christopher Bird, op. cit.

19. Perhaps the best source of information on 'auras' and Kirlian photography is S. Krippner and D. Rubin, eds., *Galaxies of Life: The Human Aura in Acupuncture and Kirlian Photography* (Gordon and Breach, London, 1973).

20. See, e.g., Shafica Karagula, M.D., *Breakthrough to Creativity* (De Vorae, Los Angeles, 1967).

CHAPTER IV *A New Medicine?*

1. John Powles, 'On the Limitations of Modern Medicine', *Science, Medicine and Man*, 1 (London, 1973), p. 19.

2. Rashi Fein, 'On Achieving Access and Equity in Health Care', *Milbank Memorial Fund Quarterly*, vol. 50, no. 4 (October 1972), pp. 158–95.

3. George B. Leonard, 'How We Will Change', *Intellectual Digest* (New York, June 1974), p. 15.

APPENDIX I *Three Essays on the Changes We Are Facing*

1. Shafica Karagula, *Breakthrough to Creativity* (De Vorae, Los Angeles, 1967).

2. Saxton Burr, *Blueprint for Immortality* (Neville Spearman, London, 1972).

3. See Andrew Weil in *Psychology Today* (New York, June 1974).

4. For full details, see Andrija Puharich, *Uri* (W.H. Allen, London, 1974).

APPENDIX II *The May Lectures: An Overview*

1. Andrija Puharich, *Uri* (W.H. Allen, London, 1974).